You Can Be Psychic Too

A comprehensive guide to becoming a medium,
clairvoyant and psychic healer

Molly Ann Fairley

The Light Network

The Light Network
Published 2013 by The Light Network

www.thelightnetwork.com

ISBN: 978-0-9571596-1-7

Edited by Keidi Keating (The Word Queen)

Layout by Danielle Raine

*I dedicate this book to you to open your heart
and soul to the loving force of spirit.
To the immense joy you will feel when you connect
with the Light and know the reason you were born!*

What Others Are Saying About This Book...

"Amazing information explained in a simple but powerful way and it is like Molly Ann is talking to you directly! You can feel the learning and healing coming from the pages clearing any doubts you have about your ability to become psychic as you turn the pages—something I have never experienced from any other book I have read."

- Ann Parker, Animal Communicator

"This book is so powerful, I could feel the healing moving through me as I read the pages. The layout of the book ensures that you find what you need when you need it. I use the angels chapter daily to help me connect to the correct angels and guides in addition to understanding so much more about the psychic world."

- Kerry O'Brien, Lady Mc

"This is a profound yet easy to absorb book, where Molly Ann guides you through your own psychic discovery within; something we all possess. The healing is literally embedded in the text. The person you shall become after reading it will be nothing short of amazing. Are you ready for the ride of your life?"

- Jay Davidson, TV Marketing Manager

"An easy-to-read book that's full of clarity and honesty of expression. Molly Ann leaves no stone unturned in explaining everything you need to do in order to develop your psychic powers. If you are serious about working psychically, this book is really unputdownable!"

- Gill Sidebottom, Reiki Master and Healer

Table of Contents

A Psychic Reading

Imagine you have booked an appointment with me for a soul reading and a psychic healing. Let us pretend that you have made the journey to my house in south west London. It is a beautiful day and the drive here was easy. You knock on my bright red door and smell the beautiful lime green tree just in front of it, which is waving its branches beneath the warm sunshine and blue sky. The red and green colours make you feel good for they compliment one another. You feel ever so excited because you have decided to have a soul reading to reveal more about yourself and to discover your potential to develop psychically. Perhaps you will find the answers about your life experiences that you have been waiting to hear for a long time; some good, others not so good. These answers may focus on why you have incarnated to the Earth plane and what you have agreed to experience here. The answers might also revolve around the people you know, those you have lost and why your life has unfolded how it has.

I open the red door and once inside I ask you to remove your shoes before I take you upstairs into a lovely lounge. The large room is illuminated with bright sunshine and it has large windows overlooking an apple tree. You wonder if you are really in London. The room is a soft shade of cream and you find yourself sinking into a cosy armchair. You can already sense the peace all around.

We look directly into one another's eyes and you instantly feel that I am searching deep inside you, looking for something, perhaps a secret that you have not yet unlocked. You have a series of questions which you want answered – questions about your life, your family, your love prospects, career, health, psychic potential, past lives and your destiny. You want answers that will free you from some of the events, people and circumstances that have made your life difficult up until now. Things that have held you back from succeeding, creating more money, changing your life, improving your relationships, or just feeling happy.

Why has your life unfolded as it has? What karma is being played out with friends and relatives? Why are your finances in such a state? Perhaps you have unresolved health problems, weight problems, addictions, irrational fears, or loneliness and you do not even know why.

This book will help you to develop psychically and spiritually and open you up to become a medium. It will also address many issues that have held you back from becoming the "real you." The real you is calm, grounded, poised, confident, able to unleash your powerful inner potential and live every moment in a state of flow. This all may sound a bit far-fetched but the real you is much closer to the surface than you realise. You are about to gain a great deal of knowledge and get in touch with this amazing potential inside.

Psychic and Past Life Stories

Throughout this book you will find a number of fascinating psychic and past life stories and at times it may feel like you have had similar experiences. Many of your spiritual brothers and sisters have come to reveal the way forward. They have chosen to help you to heal, grow psychically and spiritually, receive healing energies and learn from their experiences. Use their stories to uncover knowledge about yourself. You may even find that your own issues dissolve into the stories.

The psychic healing energies contained within these pages will first help to heal you, open up your psychic channels and then spread out to your family, friends, partners and acquaintances like a wonderful wave of warmth, embracing every soul you know with their vibrant rays. This is a natural sequence. You are the "centre pin" and everyone around you will be positively affected by your healing.

3

Now imagine you are back in that soft cream arm chair again, all cosy and warm and holding your favourite drink. Read on as I talk about spiritual enlightenment and how it goes hand in hand with your psychic and soul journey.

Spiritual Enlightenment

I expect you have heard the word "enlightenment" frequently spoken in spiritual circles as many people search to achieve the state. When we reach enlightenment we believe we can rest at last, feeling as if we have gone as far as we can go; the ultimate state of being if you like. However, has it ever occurred to you to question what the true meaning of enlightenment actually is? Do you, like many, believe that enlightenment is a paradise which you will find full of light and peace? Or is it a state of bliss, or a sense of relief at "going home?" Although all these meanings sound very attractive, none of them accurately indicate exactly what enlightenment is all about.

The truth is, it will not make any difference how psychic you become, how much you serve others, how high you fly spiritually, how many prayers you send, or how full of light you are, there will always be another level to ascend to, another level of enlightenment to reach. As humans, unless we are ascended masters or avatars in physical form, or we have heightened spiritual qualities, we are quite a long way down the spiritual ladder of enlightenment on planet Earth. Here, we are still living a consciousness of self first and sharing second. We self-harm through drugs, drinking and overeating. We hurt others through theft, dishonesty, the abuse of cheap labour and child trafficking, not to mention the sad slaughtering and eating of our animals. However, we do, thank goodness, also have the positive emotion of love, which is certainly gaining momentum.

There are also many more enlightened dimensions surrounding us – dimensions and advanced races that you could psychically travel to on your journey to enlightenment once you know how. All around us there are spiritual guides, ascended masters, millions of angels and a vast network of God's Divine helpers. You have, however, incarnated into a human body on Earth with lessons to learn to enable you to grow. If you are an old soul, you might not have learned those lessons easily and you may have needed many lifetimes to finally get where you are today. Becoming psychic could be the next step for your growth, but it is only one part of the overall picture of your soul's evolution to the higher planes. Many psychics get "stuck" in their gifts and do not move on spiritually. They experience problems with their bodies and they can have weight issues. With this thought in mind, what can you do to develop as efficiently and easily as possible?

The first realisation is that you do not actually need to go anywhere to experience enlightenment or self realisation. It is an internal state of "being" rather than a "doing" action. Enlightenment is about already having all the knowledge and ability within to cope with whatever happens around you. It means turning that negative voice inside you right down. It means you are able to overcome obstacles placed on your path and convert them into love. It means you can harness internal and external energies and add love, light and harmony to all that surrounds you. It also means that you can transform the part of you that does not believe you can be incredibly psychic, a great healer and of immense service to others. Energy is constantly changing. This is a fact. Your energy never stays the same and neither do you. You are changing and growing the whole time and because of this, there is no upper limit to your growth.

You May Choose Not to Be Born Again

Of course, when you reach a certain level of light and understanding, you may choose not to be born again onto the Earth plane. Perhaps you are actively thinking of a get-out clause right now and working out how to do it, especially if you have had a tough time so far. However, every single time you rise above something, no matter how small, you are burning your karma. You will become psychic and you will get good at it. If you are already psychic you will become even more adept, and you will be given the courage to help and heal many others if that is what you choose. All you need to do is ask God for help. If after reading this you still have an inner voice full of doubts, continue reading and you will receive healing to dissolve them.

Instead of doubting, maybe you are dealing with the other end of the spectrum where the psychic messages are coming through thick and fast and Spirit will not leave you alone. If this is you, I will teach you how to switch the psychic power on and off when it suits you. It is important that Spirit serves you and does not overwhelm you. Some spirits are very impatient when it comes to getting messages to their loved ones on Earth and they will not think about whether that is convenient for you. They can be needy and it is important that you are able to control this.

Later, at the end of your lifetime, other dimensions could offer you more opportunity for growth and radiance elsewhere than here on Earth. Earth is only a tiny planet in a universe surrounded by many other universes. Despite this, you may choose to come back here again to bring more light to others through greater service. Either way developing and greatly heightening your intuition will hold you in good stead for your future.

Your Soul Contract

Many people believe that choosing our life's path is entirely optional and that we have complete free will, able to direct our life anyway we choose. This belief is fine, but I prefer to acknowledge that there may have been definite guidelines laid down by you and the board of the Lords of Karma. The Lords of Karma are the powerful angels residing above the Archangels in the Angelic Kingdom who decide your fate together with you. Let us, for the sake of argument, assume that before incarnating, a plan has been mapped out for you. The plan will take into consideration what you need to experience in this lifetime and with whom. Spiritual contracts will have been set up at specific stages of your life and any good astrologer will be able to tell you about the dates and times of these contracts. It is said that before birth and after death we go before the board of the Lords of Karma. The Lords of Karma are responsible for holding together the entire history of humanity – the Akashic Records – so they know all about you. The Akashic Records are the files held in the ethers about everything you and everyone else has ever experienced. The Law of Karma is the law of cause and affect, the balance sheets of accountability for every action that you take and every reaction it causes in others.

Together with the Lords of Karma, you will elect to experience specific things and meet certain people while you are alive. These people will agree to live significant events with you. They could include your husband, your lover, your mother, father, siblings, school teacher, employer or bank manager and so on. Before incarnating you agree on your gender, country of birth, your parents and your social and material background. Your life plan is laid out. What you do with that plan, how it unfolds during your life and the decisions you make due to the circumstances and challenges thrust upon you, determines your soul path. All your actions are assessed at your death and a future lifetime plan is made until you finally reach enlightenment.

Your Psychic Destiny

Now you might be asking, "What has this got to do with developing psychically and how does it affect me?" Well, it has a great deal to do with your psychic development. If your destiny is to develop psychically or become a medium or healer, you will have made contracts with spiritual teachers, books, films and soul mates to receive personal guidance to ensure you carry out the plan. Part of the plan may also be that you possess a fascination with the occult or that you already enjoy being highly intuitive. Part of the plan could be that you have grave doubts about your ability so you are challenged to overcome those doubts to make you stronger. You may feel driven to grow spiritually as your soul urges you forward. You may also have elected to have a beautifully open heart as you want to help and serve others. It is likely that you are sensitive to the needs of the planet.

Psychic Past Lives

I have definitely been psychic many times before in past lifetimes. I know this because I have clairvoyantly seen those times in great detail. I can also recall my birth and conception. I did not always "know" these things. My past lives and birth memories unfolded as I developed. I obviously elected to be able to "see" past lives and ancestral lineage in both myself and others before I incarnated. This has helped me and many others to unravel why things have been as they are. This ability is clearly marked in my astrological chart. Perhaps you also had a similar background and past lives that supported your psychic development now, although this is uncertain unless you can

8

remember them. It could be your first incarnation as a developing psychic in which case you will need to be patient with yourself as you cannot force the pace.

I also know that I incarnated to serve and I have seen and emotionally experienced many times when I was not able to do so in the past. I died in great frustration and pain a number of times while watching others suffer and being powerless to stop it. Like many others I have also experienced being the perpetrator of crimes against humanity and this time I am here to learn to serve without ego. My mother in this lifetime has accompanied me on many occasions in the past and it seems that this is the first lifetime where others have not been suffering all around us. Thank goodness that this time I am on the other side of the fence, bringing healing and relief. For me it has been a very long journey.

My vast number of psychic past lives has given me a useful head start. As I have been a spiritual teacher before, spiritual teaching came to me remarkably easily this time around. I wasn't nervous about it at all and despite never teaching before the age of thirty-five, it came naturally to me. I am telling you this so you can access where you think you are on your life path and choose your next steps carefully to develop properly. Please also take into consideration your past. If you look at your circumstances, it will be fairly easy to see what you need to do. Assess the people around you and how you relate to them. Assess the type of work you have been doing and whether or not it feels right. Note whether you are able to leave that work, or if you need to stay for financial reasons. If so, what are you learning about yourself and your approach to money? Do you believe you wouldn't have any money if you worked as a psychic? You may need to access the fear you have and heal it if you wish to be a professional psychic or medium. Assess your partnerships as well and notice how they unfold. Measure your psychic knowledge, how far you have come and how much time you have donated to developing spiritually, to form a clearer picture.

You Can Choose Your Psychic Path

When you decide to develop psychically, choose the path that makes you feel well. If you only wish to learn for learning's sake then do so, as it may be that your soul wants to dabble in preparation for a future assignment. If you wish to add psychic development to other abilities then please do so. Your soul may be allowing you to begin to gain confidence in many areas before choosing a spiritual assignment later. If you wish to become a professional psychic or medium and you truly know that this is your life path then do whatever it takes to get there. You will have at your disposal a profession full of love, gratitude and spiritual evolution and, although challenging, you will grow rapidly. If you are already good at intuitive knowings and you enjoy being able to access psychic information, it is a very likely option for you to pursue. With each lifetime we are given a number of gifts to use. Some people are given lots and others less. You may even choose more than one path. There is no right or wrong way to grow and move forward. Do whatever feels right for you.

Try not to put yourself into a box. Be open to whatever happens and use the circumstances, instead of avoiding them due to emotional discomfort. The world is changing very quickly. For example, there are many more mixed marriages than ever before. In my youth this would have been unheard of, but now it is quite common.

Nowadays, people change jobs more frequently too. Self-employment is rising and the idea of having a job for life is old hat. The divorce rate is very high despite the fact that many believe this is wrong and that people should stay married forever. Nevertheless, the divorce rate is still climbing and it seems destined to continue. Marriage may well be something that many people feel boxes them in. I believe the divorce rate is high because we are all burning and cancelling karma far faster than our ancestors. We change jobs more often and move house many more times than our parents. We send emails and communicate with one another hundreds of times faster than we did even five years ago.

Many souls need to meet, interact and fulfil their karma more rapidly with others. What would have taken our grandparents sixty years to achieve is now taking place in just a few years, or even months. People need to move around and be free to go their own ways. They need to meet their twin flames, their soul mates and their soul challengers and work through the karma. The children being born could have karma with more than one father or guardian and need the stimulus of the challenges to strengthen and grow. Many of them now know all of their grandparents as people are living longer; this was not so common before.

Opposition From Others

As a developing psychic you could come up against opposition from your family, partner or friends as you learn because they may not believe in what you are doing. It can also be daunting and unnerving for someone close to you to see the huge changes taking place in your life as they could feel like they are being left behind. You may even need to really leave them behind as your paths veer in different directions and the karma ends. This can be equally frustrating and painful for you both and you might have to weigh up whether or not you will stay with a partner or certain family members or follow your spiritual and psychic path. I have seen this happen to a great deal of spiritual people.

Your soul could be asking you to stand firm about your psychic pathway, develop courage and overcome any obstacles. One of the best psychics I know had to overcome huge amounts of opposition from her family. At first, she was naive and very young. She persisted through many ups and downs until she finally broke through her karma and she is now helping thousands of people worldwide. Had she given in to her family's demands and not stood her ground, her destiny and the destiny of all those souls she had agreed to help would not have fulfilled. It took great courage on her part over many years. She is now at peace with herself because she has openly embraced her psychic gifts.

Developing psychically does not necessarily mean you will leave a loved one behind, but it will change you so please be aware of that. If someone is inflexible around you, that will prove very challenging. In this case diplomacy and understanding another's view is the best way forward, even if that is not easy for you. Try not to criticise or make them feel as if they are behaving wrongly. Your family or your partner could be feeling fear. Their fear is more than likely a reflection of your own unconscious doubt.

Grow more certain about yourself, your path and your ability and they will become calmer. This challenge may even have been placed for you to resolve and rise above. Sometimes it may look as if you will actually separate. Separations can sometimes occur in order to re-ignite the relationship, something that has been mapped out for you both to grow. It is a bit like climbing a ladder, one of you separates and the other one shifts and then you re-unite. But at the time you will not know that the separations are temporary. Each time they will feel permanent, very real and very painful.

Separations are often appropriate when two souls are evolving and they have made a contract to grow together. The moment of "letting go of the relationship and handing it over to God" is usually the deciding factor. Detachment or the acceptance of letting go of someone is often all that is required for you both to move onto a higher plane.

If you are confused about what action to take, go into your heart and listen to what it has to say. Your heart will guide you more than your head, which can get mixed up with all the thoughts whirling around inside. Before going to bed, place any questions you have about your life deep in the middle of your heart and ask it to deliver its response. It will respond with feelings and emotion rather than logic. If your head does not agree with those feelings, systematically write out all the reasons for and all the reasons against the situation and see what your head comes up with. Weigh up the answers from both your heart and your head and see if you can reach a conclusion. If you are still undecided, you may need more time to resolve any residual inner conflict.

Others Are More Psychic Than Me

Do you have pre-conceived ideas about levels of evolution? Do you think others could be more psychic than you? I have witnessed spiritual snobbery amongst those in New Age circles who often see themselves as superior to others. This is, of course, a passing phase triggered by the ego of these people who, when they have grown spiritually, will come to realise that any negative judgement of another or even yourself is a reflection of an unknown psychic energy block within. If you are comparing yourself with others, seeing yourself as less able and sending negative messages about being psychic, read on for we will deal with this later. Any ego messages like "I am not as good as others" or "I am not good enough" do not come from your soul. They come from a state of worthlessness and fear of growing and they can be healed.

4

Judgement

Judgement is difficult to control as we all need to be able to judge in order to survive. However, persistent negative judgement of another can lead you up the garden path. You do not know another soul's journey. You do not know if someone has come to Earth to learn to become a psychic or a healer, or if they are here to make heaps of money because they have lost loads in the past. Judging these souls as materialistic is pointless. In an extreme case, there is no way of knowing whether a soul is destined to become a dictator or a corrupt politician to set up certain world events. Conversely, a soul may have come to learn about being a victim, worthlessness and suffering. A soul may have even incarnated to commit suicide, or they may be here to learn to put themselves first; something which may make them seem selfish to you.

Some of the people you meet will drive you forward in a way that could be either amazingly wonderful or hugely painful. If you are critical and too fixed in your judgements you could hold yourself up by trying to prove your point. To develop psychically it is better to loosen your approach and weigh up your need to judge another. What is your need? In your eyes what have they done wrong? Heal what you think they have done wrong then move on as quickly as possible and return to your psychic studies.

Many highly developed souls have very simple jobs. They work in every area of society to bring in more light wherever they find themselves. Their soul contract is to go unnoticed as their ego does not require recognition or payment for their services. Perhaps they are balancing past life misdeeds, perhaps they have been famous in previous lifetimes and this time it is not important for them to be seen. Who knows these answers?

Their soul does. On the other hand, other highly developed souls will need recognition to get the word out there. They may have agreed a spiritual contract to reach many thousands of people during their lifetime and they will undergo all of the trials and tribulations that this brings. They may have agreed for an easy time so that it all falls into their lap.

We are all different and that is why judgement, although normal for us, is a waste of energy unless it is used to show us where we need to grow ourselves. Judging yourself is even more time-consuming. If you are having those "not feeling good enough" negative thoughts, they will stop you from becoming a confident psychic. Self-judgement will make you worry about yourself, increasing your self-consciousness and concerns about your ability. You will not be able to see the needs of others as easily as you would without it.

Penelope's Story

The story of Penelope's need to judge herself may help you. Penelope heavily judged her need to keep standing up to her bosses and she thought she had an attitude problem. She was always "rocking the boat." She saw unfair behaviour all around her at work, which made her blood boil. Eventually, Penelope would be forced to go to management to put an end to the suffering she saw. She was not always backed up as invariably her line managers were the source of the problem. On occasions, she could feel animosity and hatred coming towards her in the form of psychic attack. It took great courage for her to go above her immediate managers and state her concerns.

Distressed and confused, she came to me for a psychic reading and she was given the full picture by spirit. Her guides could not wait to come through. Penelope had made a contract to help others before

15

incarnating. She had agreed that she would disperse abuse on the work front for those less fortunate than herself. She had been doing this type of spiritual work for her last three lifetimes and she was learning to trust her intuition and increase her levels of courage. She was also learning to trust that she was being guided and supported.

Penelope had been constantly changing jobs and it was amazing how this had panned out for her. She would always end up in yet another managerial position where her members of staff had low self-esteem. They were badly treated and then made redundant with poor pay outs. The people were, of course, always very frightened of losing their jobs and, because of this great fear they had become terrified and submissive. In each case they were being bullied by a cruel and spiteful boss. Fortunately, after her first reading, Penelope returned to see me whenever it happened again and she would then receive a Divine healing for everyone.

Much of the disturbance and fear came from the past lives of all the individuals involved who were burning off karma. Many of them had mistreated others in the past and their karma was destined to be permanently healed during this lifetime. After each healing, Penelope would return to work the next day to a calm atmosphere after the fear had been lifted. The cruel boss would be either reprimanded or face dismissal. The now calm Penelope would happily hear news of her redundancy, collect her redundancy pay and leave. A new and better position would miraculously appear very shortly after so Penelope was never out of work.

Spirit clearly told me that there would always be another job for Penelope and that she had elected to be a temporary office light worker before incarnating. They also told me that each of her jobs would be better paid and an improvement on the last. Each new position would give her more financial stability and greater courage as she learned to stand up for herself and reach vaster numbers of people to change their lives for the better. Before Penelope had her reading she did not know this and naturally she had found it difficult to keep changing jobs. Armed with this new spiritual knowledge, she carefully looked back over her career. We both laughed when she realised that she was definitely being guided. She openly embraced the changes and then went with the flow, mindful of periodically collecting a nice fat redundancy cheque, a week off and an inevitable salary increase.

5

Your Psychic Pathway

You do not need super-human abilities to accomplish your purpose as a psychic, but you must really want your psychic powers in order for them to work for you. Many developing psychics fight their gifts because they are frightened or do not wish to appear unusual and different from others. You will need to make up your own mind what you are going to do. The psychic pathway is not an easy one. It will challenge you and it will compel you to grow whether you like it or not. Mainstream people may not always treat you kindly as they will often think you are odd and cannot wait to tell you that it is all mumbo jumbo. However, others will want to be told their life story the instant they find out what you do. This can be inconvenient if you are out for the evening or having downtime. People will not always have your time or your best interests at heart. You will need to develop compassion alongside a healthy ability to set up scheduled times when you do your readings and when you are in a better position to help people.

Psychic gifts are incredibly special and I always feel grateful for all the love and friendship my gifts have brought me during my lifetime. To be able to communicate with and see beautiful angels, to see, feel and hear spirit and have their incredible support and love, and to be able to bring spirit through to help another fellow human being are truly wonderful gifts. Seeing the positive changes unfold in their lives is even more gratifying. That person will go on to heal others and they, in turn, will heal even more. Because of a healing you have done or a psychic reading you have given, the Earth will radiate more light and love which, if you wish, you can be a part of.

Train Your Focus

As a sensitive being, you have a choice. You can either focus on all the "bad" things which are taking place here on Earth right now and frighten yourself, or you can be part of the wonderful loving changes that are currently occurring all around you. Powerful, positive change is afoot. It is everywhere if you look for it. I do not have to tell you that where you put your focus minute by minute is who you will become and where your life will go. Do not beat yourself up though if you have a bad day or feel very emotional. Allow the emotions to come through and they will subside. Releasing negative thoughts and emotions is normal if you are a sensitive being who is developing spiritually and psychically.

I have two friends, one is light and happy and her life is full of outings with fun and joviality. She is an Earth elemental and loves fairies. In fact I sometimes think she is one. She loves fancy dress parties, lots of pink and she even wears fairy wings. She is surrounded by other elementals who love creativity, joy and fun. The other friend is very loving and helps people and animals in great need.

Whenever I think of the first girl I sense her fun and feel good factor, yet when I think of the second one, I feel the dramas and unhappiness of the people and the pain of the animals she helps. My energy is instantly empathising. There is nothing wrong with either of these entirely different soul paths, for they wrote different contracts. I often need to remind myself, however, where I want my thoughts to land and I have to exercise control over them if I find myself spiralling downwards by overly empathising with another's problems.

You Are Steering Your Life Path

Please note that you are steering your life in a certain direction every minute of your day. It is entirely up to you where your life goes from moment to moment. I once read that if we do not go to the toilet when we need to and we hold on, we are shortening our life because of the strain on our bladder. I would never have thought about that before, but it makes sense. Multiplied over many years, that would have an enormous effect on our health if it is true. And in the same way, if you continually mix with people who are unhappy or critical, you will become like them and you will begin to feel more and more worthless. In this case you will not make a good psychic. There is a saying: "Show me the nearest six people to you in your life and I will predict your destiny."

A good psychic or healer is calm before working and neutral during the readings and healings. If this is not possible, make sure you get a healing and deal with whatever comes up for you so that you feel well before you start work. This is crucial and it will also protect your energy.

Every person you meet will reflect something within you, either positive or negative. This spiritual feedback definitely speeds up once you open up and work psychically. Throughout these pages I will constantly impress upon you the importance of cleansing yourself after dealing with people's energy. You have no idea where those individuals have been and what has been going on in their minds before they arrive on your doorstep. I once had a young male student in a workshop in n Northern Ireland who cast a heavy black cloud over the whole group. We could all feel something very uncomfortable in the room and there was a depression in the air. Even though I took him to one side and asked him what was wrong, he hung his head, glared down at the floor and was not forthcoming. What I and the others did not know that Sunday afternoon was that he was deep in thought contemplating suicide. The poor young man killed himself the very next day.

6

Our Psychic Times

On a brighter note, in 1987 the planet began to purify under the guidance of the Ascended Master, St Germain. St Germain works under the higher guidance of The Karmic Lord, The Great Divine Director, who is a great cosmic being and above the Archangels. The Great Divine Director has been directing cosmic light rays to prevent us from destroying ourselves for over two hundred thousand years.

In 1987 something very special happened, as St Germain was given permission to use the Violet Flame of Transmutation to heal everyone, not just a chosen few. Thousands of people used the energy of the Violet Flame to transform their inner darkness and send light and energy to others. A wave of spiritual books flooded the market and brand new healing techniques infiltrated daily life. Some time later, books on angels were more widely read as more spiritual people called upon the archangels for help. Many prayed to Archangel Zadkiel to transmute stuck energy. You may also have been in contact with angels yourself. Land shifts and climatic changes predicted years ago are now occurring. The floods in New Orleans are one such example of the Earth purifying itself by washing the land of past slavery. Japan is another example of the upheaval.

More and More Psychics Are Opening

More and more people are opening up psychically. You are one of them or else you would not be reading this book. Your mind and your brain think more quickly than your parents did at your age. You only have to watch a young child with a computer game console to see that their reactions are more rapid than yours were at their age. If you watch a film that is more than ten years old, you could find yourself tapping your feet impatiently as you want it to speed up; it is too slow for you. You look much younger and you are living much longer than your parents. Forty is the new thirty. Women in their sixties are dancing on television programmes like twenty-year-old young girls, proving that the body can not only last much longer, but that a woman can still be sexual at that age. I know people in their late thirties who still have grandparents alive. If you ask an older person, most only met one or two of their grandparents when they were very young.

Large numbers of people are writing books or considering writing one as they feel they have something important to say. Some of these people are writing for no financial reward and they are happy to just serve. Only fifty years ago a very select few ever went to university, let alone considered writing a book. Now anyone can write a book if they want to. They can also go to university with the right entrance qualifications – that is, if they can afford it!

As the spiritual quickening occurs, you are speeding up and adjusting to vast amounts of creative input. You are drawing closer to the Divine, the source of all creativity. This means that psychic information can be channelled through you and other potential psychics and mediums far more easily than ever before. It also means that what took psychics five years to develop twenty years ago, you can accomplish in a matter of months or in some cases even weeks.

As the light energies increase, so too will your psychic ability. We are approaching the Golden Age of Atlantis, which begins in 2032. The Atlanteans communicated telepathically and eventually you will too. Some of you originate from Atlantis so this should be quite easy. You will naturally sense if this is one of your origins. To psychically develop it is important to fully open your heart and accept these new energies into your body and mind for they have a definite purpose; they are purifying

22

you. They are preparing you for the higher vibrations flooding the Earth.

You May Be Emotional

You may be emotional, up one minute and down the next, or you may be receiving messages that you do not understand. You could be experiencing odd dreams or premonitions. You may feel anxious, tearful, weepy and overly sensitive. You may not even know why. You could find yourself weeping in front of a film or feeling disturbed by the news. Or you could be overreacting to another's behaviour. You may want to leave your job, move to open places, be alone for longer periods of time, be free to travel, or overturn the norm – the norm for you that is.

You could be eating differently or have developed odd food allergies. You could simply have gone off some foods you used to love without knowing why, or you could be overeating yet still not feel fulfilled. You may prefer to now use chemically-free products because you cannot breathe around chemical-based products. All of this is normal. You may have become very sensitive to smell, or the tone of someone's voice. This is all a natural experience if you are developing spiritually; the cells and DNA in your physical body are changing and becoming lighter. I need only 25 per cent of the food intake I needed a few years ago and I now sleep less than five hours sleep a night.

As your psychic antennae become more sensitive and are able to transmit from the higher planes, you will become more sensitive to the vibrations around you. Loud places or people may be difficult for you. Certain places or people will make you feel uncomfortable and you may not even know why. Trust your gut instinct and stay away from the people and places that do not make you feel well. Choose to spend your time in the open air, in clear uplifting places in nature. Being in nature helps dispel the effects that computers and other technological machines have on your system. The green of the trees and grass will feed and calm your third eye chakra.

You Will Need to Look After Yourself

At this sensitive stage, it is important to look after yourself. Make sure you get enough sleep and eat a balanced, healthy diet. If the news upsets you, then notice what type of news stirs up an emotional response within you. If newspapers disturb you, look at what the disturbance is and find the emotion in your body or the response in your thoughts. You may be unaware that your energy will match these situations, if not they would not affect you. Even if you do not consciously realise this, your unconscious does. Your unconscious remembers absolutely everything, going right back to the beginning of your existence.

News about a war that upsets you may remind you of past lives when you have lived through wars and been wounded or seen others die. It may bring up the memories of your ancestors who suffered in the wars as their energy is in your DNA and your unconscious. News about the abduction of a child may upset you if you or your ancestors have had children taken away from you in past lives. Murder may have a deep impact on your emotions if you have witnessed it in previous lifetimes or if you have been murdered yourself. Difficult economical situations may worry you if you or your relatives have lost everything in the past or if you have had spent time working for a pittance.

Keep healing yourself until your reactions calm and you become neutral. This is not to say that you will be indifferent to the kind of experiences that are happening around you, it simply means you will remain calm and be unaffected by them. That way, you can go about your daily life, helping and healing others more easily. In your place of calmness you can send healing energy to anyone, anywhere in the world. You can even experience transmission meditation to help others more effectively. When you are neutral, you become one hundred times more useful to Spirit and the Ascended Masters who are overseeing the positive changes on our planet. You will feel better in yourself too. Spirit cannot channel through you if your emotions are predominantly dominated by world chaos. If newspapers continue to disturb you, throw them out and if watching the news on television upsets you, turn it off and read a positive book instead. Apart from anything else, you will find that you sleep better.

The Earth Holds Psychic Energy

I vividly remember feeling very upset whenever I saw any news about Croatia. The fear and the knowledge of the dreadful atrocities that were committed there gave me nightmares. In 1967, when I was twenty, in the midst of the swinging sixties, many of my generation rebelled. As part of my own rebellion against my parents I hitch-hiked to Yugoslavia. Hitch-hiking was relatively unacceptable at the time and it was considered extremely dangerous. I travelled with five other girls. When we arrived in what was then across the border, I felt immediately agitated and I wanted all the girls to leave. I was quite insistent, which was unusual for me back then. Instead of resting, the girls got up at the crack of dawn the next day to leave for Greece. I got no sleep that night and I experienced a weird sense of dread but I could not explain what was happening to me at the time. I was too young.

When we left, I felt relieved as we travelled miles across the country heading further south. Many years later, horrific tortures were inflicted on so many people in that country during the 1991 to 1995 war in Croatia. In 1967, my psychic antennae had tuned in, knowing about this more than thirty years before the war crimes and beatings took place. Consciously, I had no idea of this. It was as if the Earth already contained the dreadful story.

A Good Psychic is Neutral

To become a good psychic you will need to be as neutral as possible. Negative situations will be placed on your path to urge you to move forward and free yourself. When it becomes too uncomfortable to stay, you will always make that final breakthrough. The more negative the situation, the more your inner drive will rise, forcing you to overcome the limitation. Noticing these negative situations can be a very useful way of clearing and healing yourself so that you are completely neutral the next time you encounter a similar set of circumstances. This is the way forward; hiding from negativity or avoiding difficult clients who mirror you or your internal blocks will not work. The circumstances will only repeat themselves via the same people or similar types landing on your doorstep again, usually with more disturbances.

Follow the chapters on healing in this book where I show you how to heal yourself each time you come across a problem, a doubt about yourself or your psychic ability, in either a situation or with a person. In this way your psychic confidence will gradually grow, along with your self-confidence. Confidence in yourself is a vital ingredient to your success. The healings I have included are very powerful so you will experience great relief from them. Each time you heal you will become lighter and more psychic, feeling more certain of yourself and your ability. Your clients will get easier and more open and the psychic information will come through more easily and rapidly. You will open up to higher and higher guidance and more effective channelling.

7

My Own Psychic Opening

I would like you to relax and make yourself a refreshing drink, puff up the cushions and sink deeper into your armchair because I am going to tell you the story of how I psychically opened. This information will allow us to draw closer together, as you will see my vulnerability at a time when I had little or no psychic experience. As a result, I hope I am more able to guide you and help you to open up and accept your own psychic changes more easily. It is quite remarkable how we all rally round a vulnerable person, or the underdog. So long as they are open and honest about their limitations, they suddenly become human and approachable. I have always been very open with my psychic students as this makes them feel safer and shows them that they are not alone in their experiences. I also want you to see that despite everything that happened to me – and a lot of unusual things have – I have been divinely guided throughout the entire process, even when I was convinced this was not the case.

You are also being divinely guided at this time, even if you have no idea whatsoever; even if you feel alone and even if you cannot see, hear or feel your spiritual guardians yet. Spirit know everything about you, right down to what you ate for breakfast this morning. Your chosen Higher Guides are directing you at all times. If you cannot see them yet, stop for a moment and ask out loud that it be made possible for you to see them, hear them or sense them. Continue asking until you get a definite sign. When they come close, it could be very subtle, so be aware of any signs that may occur.

At the age of forty-three, having been a wife and mother for many years, I had a sudden and quite unpredictable psychic opening. The only warning I received was two days before the opening when I was visited by a slim young woman called Jane who told me she was a messenger from Spirit. She urgently explained that there was no time to waste and that I must fully prepare myself for an extraordinary event that would take place within two days. Jane told me that this event had been written in the Akashic Records and that I had agreed to it on a soul level many lifetimes ago. Spirit had, however, moved the date of the event forward for they deemed me to be ready.

This extraordinary event was to begin at exactly 8pm on Thursday evening and continue right through the night. Today was Tuesday so I did not have much time. Spiritually, Jane had been elected to be the Earth helper who would support me. This would have been fine had I known Jane, but I had never seen her before that day. I knew nothing about her, only that she had been sent by a trusted, mutual friend. Surprised, I literally bombarded Jane with question after question. What was going to happen? How would it happen? Would it hurt? How long would it take? Why me? What had I done to deserve this? I felt naturally scared. Did this make me somehow special? Or was that just an ego trip?

I knew I had become more and more fascinated with psychics and mediums throughout my life. I wondered how they did what they did and how they knew the things they knew with such clarity? Fascinated, I had attended all kinds of psychic circles and I gradually started to invite budding psychics back to my house. Small groups of spiritually like-minded people gathered to witness an invited medium enter into a deep trance, become someone else and bring through profound spiritual messages. One evening psychic surgery was performed right in front of us. It was riveting stuff.

I wondered what the neighbours would say if they knew. Would they think I was odd? I was quite sure they would, so I kept it all under wraps.

A Chinese Guide

I first met Chinese Woman a few weeks after the first spiritual meetings at my house. Chinese Woman was a Chinese Guide channelled by Stephanie, a new member to the group. Stephanie was unforgettable. She had a certain wildness about her; a powerful shamanic energy. She was a flamboyant eccentric with piercing blue eyes and shiny long brown hair. Men were captivated by her and I was mesmerised by her incredible ability to transform into a spiritual being. She would speak with a foreign accent that no one imitated and I wanted to share this with others.

Soon after meeting Stephanie, the phone began to ring with people I had never heard of telling me they did not know why but they had felt drawn to ring me. They kept asking me if a spiritual meeting of some significance would be taking place soon. I did not know what they were talking about, and yet, it was as if some unseen force from above was directing these people to ring me. Confused and still wondering how they were finding me, I eventually said "yes." I invited Stephanie to come along and speak to this select few. I felt naturally nervous and I questioned my reasoning and even my sanity. What had I let myself in for? They, on the other hand, did not seem at all perturbed. Was it just me then who was getting in too deep? At last, the day of the meeting arrived. Everyone turned up on time, which was unusual in itself. They all told me they had felt drawn to come and they did not know why. We waited silently with baited breath for what seemed ages until Stephanie (aka Chinese Woman) was ready.

At precisely 11 minutes past 11am on 11th July 1991 (which all adds up to the number 11, the master spiritual number), we heard a faint shuffling and movement taking place upstairs. Stephanie, in the guise of Chinese Woman, descended the stairs one by one as if her feet were tiny and bound. We all wanted to giggle and there were some really odd looks flying across the room as Chinese Woman entered. Stephanie, with her eyes closed, shuffled her way to a chair that had been especially put there for her.

Stephanie's whole body had taken on the air of a very old woman. Her accent was Chinese and her speech was ancient as if it came from another time. Chinese Woman addressed the group and welcomed everyone as she began to tell them why they were all there. Afterwards she opened the meeting to questions. For nearly an hour we asked question after question, some about ourselves and our own soul path, some about our families, friends' personal lives and many about the world. We were all totally spellbound. Finally, much later, Chinese Woman departed with the same shuffling sounds and slowly, with a bent back, she ascended the stairs.

A Life Changing Experience

That day changed my entire life. It was impossible to ignore what I had seen. It would not go away and neither would Stephanie. She remembered very little of what had taken place and it took some time for her to return to full consciousness. I let her rest. Little did I know that she and Chinese Woman were about to play a very important role in my life and turn it entirely upside-down. There would be no going back!

Two weeks later this Jane turned up. She brought an assortment of oils and candles with her and asked me where I could spend the night comfortably. She told me that I was to be opened as a psychic channel and trance medium and that I would be able to perform psychic surgery and heal others. She also said that I would be clairvoyant and be able to bring important news to others and that later I would become a metaphysical teacher and writer and I would travel the world. She said I would be the perfect teacher of psychic healing, psychic studies and mediumship. Because I had not been born psychic, this would help me to relate to others in the same boat.

At that moment, it all seemed too far-fetched. I was frightened and in a complete daze. I had just undergone a divorce and I was only just recovering from the intense fear and identity crisis of going from a typical middle class Surrey housewife to a single woman earning her own living. I also had a fourteen-year-old daughter, who clearly wouldn't be able to fit in with all this odd spiritual stuff.

My Past Lives

Jane asked me to lie down and told me that the "opening process" was about to begin. I lay down nervously. Almost immediately I began to see images whirling around my mind; images of my life and my childhood, images of lives I had never seen before, at first vague but then brightly coloured. I shivered with cold in front of an open fire, wrapped in a thick blanket. One moment I was freezing cold and shivering, the next I was hot and sweaty. Jane brought me water and more blankets as my temperature soared up and down.

Throughout the night, I saw lifetime after lifetime, over eighty in all. I saw each of my deaths and the decisions I had made at the end of each lifetime. I saw all the events that had led to those decisions and I saw all the people – some of whom I have met in this lifetime as well. I saw skins being shed from my body and changes happening to my hearing. At times it felt like someone was operating on me with a team in the background. I could hear them talking to each other in spirit, issuing each other instructions. I was drifting in and out of consciousness. Bits of me were being connected to other bits and new bits were being put in too.

At times I found myself in physical or emotional pain. Physical injuries from the past were remembered, rapidly dissolving as they left my body. Emotions such as fear, sadness, anger and futility came up and passed through me in waves. Emotion after emotion built up inside me before breaking out in great sighs or gut-wrenching tears. It was a similar experience to giving birth. By 6am I was exhausted and very confused. Jane told me it was over and then she left. I slept until 9am when my boyfriend came over to see me. I was very tearful and in shock and I told him about the images I had seen. By this time images of Christ had started flooding through. It was my forty-fifth birthday and I no longer knew who I was and neither did he. It was a very difficult time for us both and sadly we decided to separate for some time to adjust.

The next two months were a difficult period of my life. I was unable to cope with much sound so I needed to stay near to the house. One day after six weeks had passed, I vividly remember going to Brighton on the south Coast of England and not being able to stay near the beach. I was driven right to the top where the pavement overlooks a small fairground on the front. The noise was deafening and I had to come home. Light overwhelmed my eyes and I became sensitive to the slightest change. I kept the curtains closed for weeks. Physically I felt more tired than I had ever been, even in late pregnancy. On the odd trip out, I would need to sit on walls after short walks, rather like an old lady.

Psychic Energy Flashes

Daily, I saw energies flitting past my eyes and out of the corners of my eyes; they looked like tiny sparks. My emotions were sensitive and raw. I could feel people's energy, moods and thoughts through my stomach, which was totally new to me. I instantly knew if someone was being dishonest. My intuition had been cranked up hundreds of times and I just seemed to "know" so many things that I did not know before. It was as if I had one mind in my head and another in my stomach. I could feel where my aura started and stopped, where it was picking up information and how it was constantly moving. Sometimes I saw colours too, but I had no idea what they meant. It all felt so new to me.

In the midst of all this Stephanie moved in. She arrived one day about a week after "that night" carrying a small brown leather suitcase and a message from Chinese Woman. She was to stay for two months until I was well. Well? I did not know that I was ill, but apparently so. Stephanie told me she had channelled that I had undergone a huge spiritual frequency conversion (a strange description I thought) and that it had shaken me emotionally and physically, right to the core of my being.

Unknowingly I Had Been Prepared

Apparently my body had been prepared for this spiritual conversion for years, which was news to me, but it had still proved an enormous shock to my body and my mind. I was told it would take time to heal. I remembered I had thought it strange that I suddenly studied yoga at the age of thirty so intensively and rapidly became a teacher after having only ever worked in an office throughout my life.

What I found even stranger was that this happened because of a series of nervous breakdowns that had called an abrupt halt to my then over-zealous need to work all the hours God provides. No doctor or specialist seemed to be able to fathom out the cause of these breakdowns. On the allotted day, however, I remember finding a book called *Peace from Nervous Suffering* by Dr Claire Weekes. On page 87 I found the answer to my nervous breakdowns. I read it, understood what she was saying and then I was cured.

Now, all these years later, it all fitted together like a jigsaw puzzle, with all the pieces in place. Without the gruelling workouts and mental ordeals I had endured whilst training to be a yoga teacher, I would not have been fit enough to have sustained the frequency changes or mentally strong enough for the emotions to flow.

It was a relief to have Stephanie living with me. She was light-hearted and fun to be with. She took over the cooking and the housework, leaving me able to ask as many questions as I wished. She told me that food would be provided as I could not leave the house. Food was delivered to the door each day, which she said came from Spirit. I never did find out who the real Earth benefactor was.

She told me light-hearted stories about Spirit and the playful things the baby Earth Spirits like to do. Under the constant guidance of Stephanie and, on occasion, Chinese Woman, I felt thoroughly supported and spoiled. Stephanie spoke in riddles or stories when she wanted me to learn something, which kept me guessing. I was often made to wait for the answer until I knew it myself intuitively. This strengthened me and heightened my ability to work psychically and intuitively. Miraculously, within five weeks of Stephanie's arrival, I was conducting psychic surgery as a trance medium and bringing through messages in front of small groups.

8

Are You Psychic?

So far, I have briefly talked about mediums and trance mediumship because that is what I experienced when I first became psychic. My opening experience was unusual and I have never met anyone else in all the years that I have been teaching who has gone through such a sudden and dramatic psychic experience. They have gone through upheaval and change and their approach to life has been altered a great deal, usually in a positive form, but they have never endured the shock and trauma I went through. Most psychics or mediums are born with their abilities or they open gradually at a pace which is comfortable for them.

A Psychic is Not the Same as a Medium

A psychic is not the same as a medium. If you lean more towards being a psychic than a medium, you will tend to clairvoyantly see a situation, or hear or sense an issue which has been brought to you. You will have a sense of your own awareness and often a view to resolving it in some way. You would, of course, be able to receive information from Spirit, but it is likely to come from spirit guides as opposed to those who have passed over. It may seem as if it is your own voice talking to you in your head.

Some psychics receive a constant flow of information and if you were to ask them during a reading how they know what they do, they would not be able to tell you. They are quite capable of knowing what is going to happen in the future and being able to tell you why something is taking place in your life, but they are not knowingly communicating with anyone. They do not see guides, spirit or angels, they just transmit psychic information. It is rather like having a conversation, but you would talk about the future or the past with as much ease as you would talk about the present. If this sounds like you, you would be fully conscious just knowing things. It is a bit like talking to a friend as ideas pop up in your mind easily and effortlessly. This type of psychic is quite happy to receive their gift for it is normal to them and because of that they make excellent readers.

Sometimes information is transmitted from an alien source and when it comes through it can be very matter of fact and never emotional. I once clairvoyantly saw a sort of Morse Code in light come towards me in waves and I realised it was alien in origin. When the waves arrived, I waited, aware that a translation was taking place. I then telepathically received information through words.

You May Have Come Through Reiki or Healing

You may have noticed that you do not fit into either of these two categories; a medium or what I call a "matter-of-fact psychic," as you may be developing different psychic skills. If you have come to psychic development through Reiki or spiritual healing, or because you have a deep inner drive to help others, you may be given information about a person's health as opposed to receiving psychic information about their future. You may also sense this information rather than see or hear it.

I have known psychics who are only experts in delivering messages about a person's health or weight. They can literally see into people's bodies and adjust their health problem on the etheric plane, invoking a physical healing. If they are more sense orientated they can feel the illness or pain and able to move it through their own body and out again. These psychics are extremely useful as they often unravel health or weight issues that no one else could resolve.

Psychic Healing

Psychic Healing is different from spiritual healing or Reiki. It is very specific and heals exact situations rather than just sending energy. Psychic Healing is the use of psychic forces to clear and dissolve specific issues. When working with psychic healing, I look for the exact causes of the problem, sometimes which trace back into the past. It is not general in its nature. I may have to look into the ancestral lineage or I may access several past lives and dissolve the karmic outcomes. I might need to find the part of the person that has the problem. We often have many parts and inner children, not just one.

With psychic healing, it is possible to ask for precisely the spirit who needs the healing on the other side. I have witnessed amazing psychic healings take place in spirit. They do not take place on this Earth plane but in the spiritual ethers. When accessing the Akashic Records, it is possible to know exactly where to go to invoke a healing. I am also told which of the higher beings are involved. Sometimes it is the angels, sometimes the spirit guides, sometimes the relatives over the other side, or someone alive here. It is a very powerful process.

Groups of people can be psychically healed either by speech pouring through at a rapid speed from Spirit or by quietly thinking about the specific problem. I have conducted large spiritual weight loss and other groups in this way and the shifts are amazing.

Powerful Psychic Healers

I once saw a young Russian girl on television who was about nineteen-years-old. They called her "the miracle worker," as she had the amazing gift of looking into people's bodies and diagnosing their problems when no doctor and surgeon could do so. A long queue of excited people stood in front of her waiting for answers to questions about their health that they had not been able to unravel for years. Once diagnosed, they felt great relief. This girl worked very rapidly needing only ten to fifteen seconds to be able to make a complete diagnosis.

I have also witnessed a man of twenty-two who knows exactly what is taking place in someone's body – he can see it, sense it, hear it and heal it, while having a simultaneous conversation with someone standing next to him or across the room. "Goodness," you might say to me. "Can he really work properly?" The answer is a definite, "Yes!" He really can do all those things at once. The uncertain part of me watched him for some time to make sure of that answer. As I watched him, fascinated, I realised that he worked better when he was distracted allowing the spiritual energies to do their work by passing through without much input from him. His spiritual guardians needed him out of the way so that he became a pure channel.

I found it worked the same for me so I was relieved to see another person working in a similar way. When healing someone, the energies seem to work much better if I am occupied with gardening, walking or cooking. In my case conversing with others does not work because for me healing nearly always comes through in clairaudience. I hope you find this as fascinating as I do because it completely quashes the idea that we have to be totally concentrating and partially tranced out to do psychic work. Sometimes it is better to take the accelerator off and let the car freewheel for a moment or two. Surprisingly, some of my best readings have come out after I have had a drink or two.

I have worked in the area of psychic healing for many years and I have also worked in past life regression. This may well feel right for you too. You may hold a fascination for gaining this knowledge or by developing into a psychic or medium who can read past lives for others. Psychics who are skilled at past life regression have usually accessed many of their own past lives before becoming psychically able to do this for others. Please notice if this feels right for you. Are you beginning to uncover memories from the past? Do you sense people who you may have known before because they feel familiar?

Forensic Psychics

Some psychics are known for their expertise in helping the police to find evidence. I was once asked by the police in Northern Ireland if I could tell them where a man in his thirties was lying at the bottom of a large lake. He was a father with young children and he had fallen in. The police suspected suicide. However, Spirit told me it was an accident because he had been drinking. Apparently he slipped and lost control as he was very drunk. The police also asked another psychic who confirmed everything I had told them. This news helped his family enormously and took away the possibility of years of suffering for them. Suicide can take the people left behind years to get over. Also, the Irish are much more open to the world of Spirit and so they tend to believe mediums perhaps moreso than a reserved English family.

Psychic Readings and Suicide

I have had the opportunity of meeting a number of parents who have lost children through suicide. When the child comes through and explains their motive and the parent lets go of their emotion and understands, forgiveness is forthcoming and it gets healed. Everyone, both on this side and the other side, experiences peace. I have seen this even in the most dramatic of suicide cases.

On one occasion I was told that a young English girl of twenty-one had taken her own life because it was time for her to go up to the angelic kingdom and continue her work with the angels. She had already become an angel at the time when she spiritually presented herself to me at a sitting. I also got the impression that she had been an incarnated Earth angel. I gave her distressed boyfriend, whom she had left behind, a lot of healing and he understood that she now had other work to do. The Earth plane had proved too much for her sensitivity; her body and mind had not been able to cope here as the energy was too dense. She appeared to me as an angel; she looked young and beautiful and she was happy, serene and at peace. Her boyfriend had a profound realisation and after many tears he finally healed and accepted her happiness as a positive move. She had suffered greatly before her death and he finally put aside his own need.

I have heard many stories of people judging those who have committed suicide but when I liaise with spirit guides, I am always being told that there is no judgement in spirit and the distressed Soul is looked after until healing has occurred on the inner planes. The Soul can then be encouraged to return to Earth to finish the karmic agreement if and when it feels ready and strong enough.

Some psychics develop the ability to channel the higher energies and they are quite happy communicating with the Gods and Goddesses, Deities and so forth. One of my students recently developed an ability to talk with Egyptian Gods and Goddesses. She had experienced many past lives in Egypt and these Gods would visit her during the night whilst she slept. She developed very quickly and she has become an excellent psychic and medium. We are all different. Bearing that in mind, I would like you to think about yourself for a moment and see if you can sense how you will begin to develop or, if you are already psychic, how you can develop further.

9

Are you A Potential Yedium

A medium is not the same as a psychic. Mediums receive messages directly from those who are dead. Have you ever had impressions or messages from people who have passed on? Have you experienced a grandfather, father, grandmother, mother, sister, brother, aunt, or uncle who has passed but whom you can clearly feel around you? It feels as if they are still here, close by. Maybe you can almost touch them, or you might have felt a soft brushing across your face, or a sudden change in temperature around you. Spirit are very cold so they can bring the temperature in a room right down. Perhaps you have heard them talking to you. You may also have picked up impressions or messages from other people's loved ones who have passed to the other side? When you visit old places, you might tune into the feelings and thoughts of the spirit of the people who used to live there.

Spirit guides or guardians fall into an entirely different group of spiritual beings. Spirit guides are not the same as deceased people as they come from a different place, from the higher realms of consciousness, the super conscious planes and the angelic kingdoms. They are divided into many categories and I will go into these later. Earth spirits, sometimes known as Earth angels, incarnate into human beings to help the planet. You may be one of them and if you are, you will be highly sensitive to colour, your surroundings, people and their vibrations and you will be disturbed by violence of any type. You will not understand the need to fight and why people need to hurt one another. You might also avoid confrontation. When Earth angels pass on, they go to the higher spiritual planes to assist humanity from the world of spirit, continuing the healing work they did when they were alive.

Deceased Spirit

Deceased Spirit are just that...deceased. They usually still have the same personality as they did when they were alive, unless they have had to go through lessons in the world of Spirit. When they come through, they often love to present themselves as looking many years younger – usually how they appeared when they were in their prime. They rarely present themselves looking as they did when they passed over. This confused me a great deal when I first began channelling and seeing Spirit. I used to ask for a lot of confirmation from my clients, especially about hair colour. Asking did not always help though because the enquirer had often never known the "real" colour of his mother's hair.

Young-looking or otherwise, Spirit are dead and they exist on the plane of discarnate souls. Being deceased does not necessarily mean that they are any wiser than they were when they were alive, which is something that people tend to forget. They are often just as mean and nasty as they ever were. However, some of them do go to the inner planes for healing and they train to work as helpers in between their incarnations. Others do not appear to change very much from how they were when alive. Many are very loving and bring forth wonderfully uplifting messages for loved ones who are still living.

The Dead Carry Emotions

I have known many discarnate dead spirits to carry forward unresolved emotions and often a spirit has to be healed to free up someone alive on Earth to make positive changes. There can also be family karma and the person who is still alive may be paying back that karma. I have often communicated with mothers whose energy is so strong that it continues to dominate their daughters. When the deceased mother is healed, the daughter is able to change completely and she feels wonderfully free. The mother's own karma is then lifted for her to move on to wherever she is going.

Many German girls seem to have this problem. Maybe it is karma that Germany carries. I have been surprised by the number of young German women who have arrived on my doorstep with mother issues. Weight problems can go down a family lineage as well. I once did a psychic healing on the spirit of the great great aunt of a young lady who had a terrible weight problem. The great great aunt was healed of her obsession with food and the young lady immediately stopped her habit of binge eating.

Ancestors Can Control Your Issues

Many other issues, such as addictions and weaknesses, not to mention money worries, can also be psychically healed this way. Psychically bringing this information through will give you a rapid head start over more conventional methods of healing. Once you trust spirit they will do you proud and tell you things way beyond what others will be able to do.

A friend of mine recently lost her nineteen-year-old niece in a sudden death. She died in her sleep. Spirit told me that she had suffered an aneurysm (blood clot) because of the birth pill she had been taking. Her blood had thickened and congealed because she had not taken time out to have any periods and she had taken the pill constantly without a break. They also told me that her time on this Earth was up. She was an incarnated angel and had been called back to work on the other side.

Spirit Can Feel Urgent

Relaying messages from Spirit can be a bit unpredictable and sometimes even daunting so you will need to develop a strong and grounded personality to be able to do this work. Spirit can often feel urgent in their need for you to deliver a message to someone. Never allow them to overpower you. Tell them firmly that you will accept their message if they are patient and give it to you in an acceptable manner, so you do not feel overpowered when you first open up. If you are firm, they will always back down. I remember I once felt compelled to enter a restaurant on a small Greek island. I felt absolutely driven to walk into that restaurant. Although I was a little apprehensive it seemed that something was literally "pulling" me forward.

When I spoke with the restaurant owner, he immediately told me he had asked Spirit to send him a medium because he wished to speak with his wife. His wife did indeed come through and she could not wait! It was she who had been propelling me towards the restaurant in the first place. She had died three weeks earlier and she felt she had not finished the row she had with her husband before she went. Remarkably, she continued to nag him, only this time from the other side. The restaurateur was visibly shocked by the argument and had not expected me to arrive in my bright pink T-shirt with a dazzling motif on the front. A visit to his local spiritual church would have been more in tune with his expectation. I also did not expect to be relaying such an unpleasant message. His wife was very angry. Since that day I have learned to be more careful. Nevertheless, a healing did take place for the woman and they reconciled their differences.

If you have lost someone very near and dear to you, you will know the immense relief of visiting a medium as opposed to a psychic to receive a message from your loved one. I know mediums who know the names of members of your family or who will give you snippets of very personal information, which is very reassuring.

Your Loved Ones Are Still With You

Deeply bereaved people often tell me that the energy of their deceased partner is so great that they do not feel like they can meet someone new. It is as if their partners are still alive and if they met someone else, it would feel like a total betrayal. I even had one lady, Janet, who told me that her husband would make love to her at night. I could see that it was completely true. Her husband was visiting every evening and staying the night. When people like Janet make close and frequent contact with their loved ones, they feel loved, safe and secure.

When someone alive has lost someone close, constantly thinking about that person can keep that spirit Earthbound for longer than necessary. Although this is not wrong, it also works the other way around and you could feel overwhelmed by your dead loved one's presence. This is usually because they feel the same about leaving you behind. It may be too much for them. This is especially true of those who have passed over too early from sudden illnesses or suicides.

Sometimes the karma is so deeply entwined between two soul mates that even death will not separate them. We may not always understand this for we do not know the details of the soul contract taken out between the two individuals. All I know is that this overwhelming type of grief must take its time to heal. In cases like these, compassion, patience and understanding are needed from you as a medium.

You Become a Go Between

As a medium you will act as an intermediary between you and the dead person. I have often seen closure occur when this happens and people who arrive in deep mourning leave me feeling something profound has resolved both within themselves and the loved one they have lost. They are lighter, reassured and they often lose their guilt or anger. I have always been an admirer of the qualities I have seen in good mediums, so if you feel this could be for you, go ahead and start training. It is a wonderful vocation and the rewards are very high.

Bear in mind though, that mediumship is quite different from clairvoyance. It is the ability to talk to both the living and the dead. Mediums can also see the dead and feel them in their bodies. Sometimes a small child can be a natural medium but he or she does not always inherit this ability from a mother or father. None of my relatives has any psychic or mediumship abilities whatsoever and yours may not have either.

Suspicion

Remember that many mediums are treated with suspicion so you could be too and you might be labelled a fraud or charlatan. People also love to test you, especially those with a cynical nature. I have long held the belief that inside every cynic there is fear. If you convert a cynic he or she will be the one person who advertises you to absolutely everyone they know. They will leave no stone unturned and may well become the most loyal of your clients. I have seen this occur many times and it is really quite extraordinary.

Some people are not cynical but they need proof because that is their nature. Maybe they have had their fingers burned in the past so they have developed a careful personality. If you were selling something to them, they would be exactly the same. In fact, you are selling something; you are selling yourself. If their careful approach makes you feel irritable or uncomfortable, try to root out the cause of your feelings. If you need to prove yourself to them to match their energy, you are only playing into their hands. If you are sure of your ability, stand your ground and don't rise to the bait. If not, you are again dealing with a doubt you have within as to your ability as a medium. If this is true for you, go within and root out your doubts. There will always be a cause inside somewhere. Ask for guidance and for all your doubts to be healed. (See the Healing For Self-Doubt at the end of Chapter 12.) It is likely that this can be traced back to your past somewhere. When this is healed you will not attract suspicion.

The suspicion of mediums dates back to the Victorian times when people held tea party séances and viewed spiritualism as a weapon to rebel against the tight rules of the time. Most mediums still carry this stigma, however. Fortunately, modern television programmes, which feature mediums giving messages to the general public, have helped others to accept mediumship. When a large audience listens to a medium relay a spiritual message and watches the recipient accepting it as truth, it is difficult to believe the old devil worship stories associated with this wonderful craft.

10

What is a Trance Medium?

Trance mediums are a rarer breed than clairvoyants or mediums because entering trance requires a great deal of trust. If you are going to allow yourself to go into trance and be overshadowed, you will need to know that you are safe. In my psychic opening story, I told you about the psychic surgery that was performed on me by Chinese guides during a three week period. It was an odd experience as I felt very old and bent over and I could easily see inside people's bodies at all the organs. As the guide, I instinctively knew exactly what to do. My hands and fingers were moved independently like a surgeon's. They were not my hands. Obviously a higher source was working through me.

When you are overshadowed by a higher energy, it is an extraordinary experience. The guides that come through can be from all denominations. Some of the most potent spiritual messages received on this planet at this time come through trance and channelling. Trance mediums deliver powerful uplifting guidance. Many spiritual books are channelled and the authors are in a state of semi-consciousness or trance as they write their words.

In trance, information has come from the wonderful light beings from Pleiades. The special Pleiadian forces reside at a very high frequency and they see spirit guides. These guides are far more elevated than the human form, but because of their alien qualities, they are very matter-of-fact and they feel totally emotionless. I have experienced many other guides overshadowing me from different dimensions. Some bring important messages for the planet along with information about an individual's soul path. Sometimes I can hear what is being said and sometimes I can not. Strange accents pass through my lips and I can sense their amazing wisdom. Often it feels like I am being moved slightly to one side as they come through me to communicate.

When I channel doctor or healing guides the experience is frequently awe-inspiring. I once felt a German doctor come right through my body, who had lived in Gibraltar for most of his life. The specialist doctor had an urgent message for those present in the room and, as he was communicating, I had enormous medical knowledge. I also knew exactly what it felt like to be responsible and treat so many people. This doctor was different from the Chinese guides, whom I do not think had ever incarnated from the higher planes. He had lived on Earth, where he had learned his skill.

If you wish to learn to become a trance medium, it is a good idea to have hypnosis. Trance is about letting go completely. It is an altered state of consciousness, just like hypnosis. Before my own experiences with trance mediumship I had been for many hypnosis sessions. I became used to letting go and deeply relaxing, often in crowded places. During these times I trusted that I was completely safe and protected.

Trance Mediumship and You

If you wish to work in trance in front of a group, it is vital that you clear your mind and expect only the right entities to come through you. Train yourself to expect the most uplifting guidance. If you have heard negative stories about other trance mediums who have had difficult experiences, try not to dwell on them. If you feel afraid, remember that all fears are a reflection of what is going on in your mind.

In trance, your awareness will feel separate from your body. This is a unique sensation as you sort of know what is taking place, yet on the other hand you do not. Take your time at the beginning and rest afterwards until you feel complete again. Make absolutely certain that you are not touched during or after trance. Coming out of trance is a bit like coming around after an anaesthetic – you may feel disorientated or even drowsy. I once came out of trance and began to speak to people too early. As a result I felt disorientated and tired for days afterwards. That was an important learning curve for me and I never did it again.

If you like the idea of experiencing your awareness as separate from your psychical being and you want to sense energies which are far higher than your own, go ahead. Personally I think it is well worth it.

Marjorie's Psychic Opening

Marjorie was an auburn-haired Irish lady from Dublin. She left Ireland and her home when she was just twelve-years-old as her father was an alcoholic and her mother was exhausted bringing up all of her many brothers and sisters. Once Marjorie established herself, she married in England then started to climb the ladder of success, becoming an astute business woman with a flair for the ridiculous. She always went against the grain in her search for freedom.

When Marjorie (or Marj as she was more commonly known) first arrived on my doorstep, she was about to go through a divorce. She and her husband at the time had completed the karma with their business and the children they had brought into the world. She asked me if her marriage would break down and her spiritual guardians immediately told me "yes." The dreadful turmoil of mixed emotions she experienced throughout the course of the divorce opened her up psychically. Within six weeks Marjorie was able to read for others and she soon became a first-class medium and psychic. She would look into a large mirror in a state of trance and allow spiritual guides to overshadow her and impose themselves upon her face. If I watched I could see her face transfigure into that of the visiting spirit. In trance she would receive wonderfully uplifting messages, which she passed to all who needed them.

Crystals Began to Magically Talk

Crystals would magically talk to Marjorie and tell her where they wanted to go to heal someone. She would programme them, send them in the post and miracle healings would take place. Marjorie opened a beautiful shop full of the most amazing crystals I have ever seen. They were breathtaking. Sparkling crystals of every colour lit up the small shop and people came from far and wide to see them and purchase them. Marjorie had no previous experience of crystals in this lifetime and she felt no need to study under a teacher to improve her spiritual gifts. She completely trusted her amazing intuition.

Marjorie developed as a powerful medium and healer and she gained quite a reputation. By simply gazing into the mirror she could access the world of the collective unconscious and she was able to heal people far and wide. She had the power to send many hundreds of Earthbound or disturbed souls into the light at one time. Angels and fairies loved Marjorie and they frequently visited her farm. Earth spirits loved it there too for they felt safe with the animals in the grass and the surrounding trees.

I knew that Marjorie had been a high priestess in Egypt and that her health was failing. Her time to pass was approaching. Many people told me that I was wrong, but sadly I knew it was true. Shortly before her death, she decked her new home out in purple and gold, the two highest spiritual colours revered by the Buddhists. She had no conscious idea that she was dying and she grew furious with me if I ever mentioned her health or her excessive smoking. Some weeks later she died, exactly ten years after the first warning spirit gave me about her health. At her funeral we could feel her presence everywhere along with the hundreds of spiritual guides, angels and archangels who had worked through her whilst she was alive.

Marjorie has since become a busy and efficient spiritual guide on the other side. On one occasion I was with a friend when she came through from Spirit. The smell of her cigarettes nearly choked the two of us. She knew that I disliked her smoking and this was exactly the type of joke I had expected her to play on me from the other side. By doing this she was making sure I knew it was definitely her.

11

Spontaneous Psychic Openings

My story and Marjorie's story will of course be completely different from yours. Your psychic opening will be totally unique. In fact it may have happened already or perhaps it is happening gradually, without you even knowing. A sudden and unexpected opening can, however, be quite alarming as well as exhilarating, even if you have wanted this to happen for years.

My psychic opening happened nearly twenty years ago when the planetary energies were much darker and denser than they currently are. This time lapse has made a huge difference as the Earth's consciousness has lightened and speeded up enormously since then. For many people who have really burned up lots of karma, it may not feel like a short space of time especially in those dark moments. In spite of this, many thousands of spiritual people and potential psychics all over the world have continued to heal themselves and others. These special helpers have contributed to lightening the energies of the planet to allow your unique way of unfolding psychically to begin.

Sarah's Spontaneous Opening

Sarah, a gentle lady in her fifties, came to see me with several issues she wanted guidance on. Her energy felt unsettled. She told me her life had suddenly altered direction. She had studied Neuro Linguistic Programming (NLP) and had gone for a lot of healing in just a few short months despite not knowing or understanding why. NLP students are usually fairly logical so anything of a psychic nature could seem quite foreign.

Sarah soon began to tell me how she dreaded losing her mother, which was completely irrational. She could not use her logical mind to work out the reason for this and she was absolutely terrified. She told me that over the months, it had literally become an obsession, playing on her mind for most of the day. In spite of this, Sarah's mother, who was nearly eighty-one-years-old, was still alive and in excellent health.

Sarah's story instantly took me back to the death of my own mother. I vividly remembered cleaning out her kitchen cupboards one hot summer's day when she was still alive. I was confused and tearful, thinking I was having a silly turn, whilst my logical daughter kept asking me why I was so distraught. I repeatedly told her that this would be the last summer I would do this. "Don't be silly, Mum," she said as she pointed at my mum who was sitting in her favourite chair, laughing her head off at the TV. Like Sarah's mother she was also robust and healthy with no outward signs of illness at that time.

Spirit interrupted my thoughts about my mother and showed me the Akashic Records of Sarah's mother's past lives. I was shown images of a woman having her inheritance stolen by her brothers in Germany in the 16th century. Sarah jumped up excitedly and told me that this had also happened in this lifetime and that her mother had been pressured by relatives to give up her portion of the family assets.

Immediately after, I was guided to another lifetime – Sarah's most recent. Her mother had died in her arms. She and her mother had been Polish Jews imprisoned in a camp in Poland. It was bitterly cold and her mother had suffered from tuberculosis. She was wrapped up in a thick dark coat but her feet lay exposed in icy water. I asked Sarah if her mother had a chest condition in *this life-time and she confirmed with a "yes." Sarah had been only fourteen-years-old during this Polish lifetime and she knew few of the people in the camp. To lose her mother was like losing a huge part of herself. How would she survive such a dreadful ordeal and such awful conditions alone? She had become dependent on her mother. They had clung to one another for years in that frightful place only just surviving with barely enough to eat.*

Suddenly, I could vividly see a fourteen-year-old girl clutching onto her mother. She was terrified and grief-stricken, desperate to keep her alive. As I relayed what I was seeing Sarah remained completely emotionless. This is unusual because people can normally feel what is taking place from their past lives. Sarah was entirely different somehow because she remained so quiet.

When we met, Sarah was not at all psychic. She had never even met a psychic before, nor had she ever been a visual person. She knew this from the NLP trainings. She told me she did not think in pictures but mainly in words with a constant voice talking inside her head. Knowing all this, I could not help but wonder why Sarah was so quiet when I told her this very emotional news. It turns out that Sarah was subdued because she was actually witnessing the pictures I described. This was a first for her and she was in awe of the process. She was clairvoyantly "seeing" and completely unemotional because she was not participating. She was observing only the clairvoyant energies that passed in front of both of us. Finally, when the images had run their course and the session ended, she stopped worrying about her mother's death. She recognised that her mother in this lifetime was her mother in her previous life too and that she had lost her.

A very excited Sarah left me ready to enrol on a psychic development course, totally fascinated by what she had seen. She knew she had seen the images clairvoyantly as she had observed the experience, not remembered it. Psychic images are lighter than memories as you can see through them. They are different and Sarah knew it.

Healing Fear of Loss

Perhaps you have started to see images without knowing how or you may dread losing your mum or dad and do not know how you will cope. You may have lost one or both of them already and you are now having difficulty with your feelings.

If this is you, sit quietly and light a candle. Link into this story and out loud ask your spiritual guardians to align you with the powerful healing energies that Sarah received so you can be healed too. I am also sending you healing right now. Please open your heart to receive it.

12

Gradual Psychic Development

Opening psychically can also be a very gradual and gentle process. Many of my students can remember as far back as their teens and are able to relate fascinating stories about their spiritual journey. Dawn has an amazing sense of humour and she is blonde, bubbly and bright. People gravitate to her because she is so much fun. Dawn told me that when she was thirteen she began to see her plants "dance." When this happened the windows were shut so she was certain there was no wind. At first, Dawn was not sure if she was imagining this so she called her mother to have a look. Together they watched as the leaves of the plants moved and vibrated in front of them. Dawn finally got all her powers through in her fifties despite having started so young.

...

Jackie's Gradual Psychic Development

Jackie has been drawn to spiritual groups for a long time. She lives in Spain and has organised Spiritual Festivals for many years. Jackie has helped many people to improve their careers and spiritually connect with one another. She is a lovely, warm, dark-haired Irish girl. Jackie learnt to meditate and chant and she has read widely on spiritual matters, being particularly drawn to books on angels. She has also been involved with Buddhism and has had lots of spiritual healing and readings. She has also spent many years developing psychically and she has learned the Tarot as well.

I first met Jackie what seems like ages ago on a radio programme. She was quietly sitting outside the radio station and told me she had been sent to meet me. I wondered if it was going to be another one of "those" meetings after my encounter with Jane and Chinese Woman.

Jackie later came for a reading and some guidance about her future. She had always been prone to money worries and she could not understand why. On linking in, I psychically saw a new flat coming in for her. It was on the first floor of a house with big windows and I saw that it would cost 32,000 Euro. Jackie was quite surprised as the idea of owning a property had not really occurred to her at that time. She knew she would one day, but had not known how she would pay for it. I told her that her spiritual guides wanted to help her and that she had good karma coming to her because of her work. I was told to tell her to pray out loud to her spiritual guardians on a daily basis to ask that this property become hers if it was meant to.

Jackie Began to See Angels

Three months later it did and so did her ability to see angels. They gradually presented themselves to her through knowledge, pictures and words entering her mind. It took Jackie many years to develop her clairvoyance fully and many more years before she actually trusted what she was being shown.

Healing Self-Doubt

Do you doubt yourself psychically? If so, are there also other areas in your life where you doubt your ability? Self-doubt usually pervades all areas of our lives if it is present. If this is the case, gaining self-esteem and eliminating self-doubt will help you a great deal as you will feel more centred and alive.

Out loud, ask your spiritual guardians to come forward and help you remove these doubts. Watch the doubts go down from your head, through your feet and into the core of the Earth where there is a magnificent fire waiting to burn them up. Keep sending them down to the fire. When they have all been burned, imagine a star far away in the galaxy pulsating rings of golden lights in all directions that balance energies and harmonise everything. One ray of starlight containing powerful healing energy crosses time and space towards you. Its rays pour in through the top of your head. You are drenched with deep golden light from top to toe. Your body is cleansed, balanced and harmonised and your mind is transformed with the pulsating rings of golden light.

Out loud, ask again that all doubts be cleansed and healed. Command that any lingering doubts be cast into the fire. Call upon Archangel Raphael to dissolve them completely. You may see a beautiful emerald green as you do this because you are invoking Archangel Raphael's energy. As the healing finalises, you will feel a new more confident you emerging. Repeat this exercise as many times as necessary.

13

Are You On a Mission?

With the changing energies and the raising of humanity's consciousness, the amount of time needed to become psychic has greatly reduced for a wide number of people. Potential psychics and mediums used to sit in circles developing for years, sometimes channelling only a small piece of information here and there. Nowadays, I have often witnessed complete novices like Georgina experiencing spontaneous psychic openings.

This is because many new devotees are needed right now to wake up those souls who are still spiritually sleeping. The Earth is undergoing masses of change and healing and so are we. Most potential psychics and sensitives feel they are on a mission to help. It is a force that lies buried deep within them. Perhaps you also sense that you have come here with something to do. It might possibly be that you have incarnated to do something special.

I have dedicated a large proportion of this book to the psychic trainees and their healing stories and psychic openings. I have also shared knowledge with you on the more conventional ways of developing. I have done this deliberately to heal any blocks you have to developing psychically and reaching your greatest potential and to understand how easily it could happen for you.

How Do You Know You Are Opening Psychically?

How do you know if you are opening psychically or just imagining it? One of the first signs I see in most people who attend my classes is that they feel drawn to come. You may feel the need to learn and absorb as much spiritual knowledge as you can get your hands on. You may begin to notice events that seem like coincidences. You could instantly feel comfortable with someone you have never ever met before, or you could meet others from past lives and just click.

Annette, a very practical student of mine and a mother of three, began to notice more coincidences than usual. She noticed that people with the same name all booked appointments on the same day. Coincidences had probably been occurring in her life for years, but without her heightened perception, she had never noticed them before. Another student frequently saw little flashes of light darting about the corner of her eyes. She thought she was suffering from eye strain, but she was seeing spirit guides.

You may experience what I call "light shimmering." It is similar to the heat shimmering you see on hot surfaces – like that you might see on a long road in a hot country, only it is light not heat. I had to leave a building when I first encountered this sight because I thought I had a problem with my eyes. I did not; I was just seeing higher energy frequencies. On other occasions I saw green energy in small clouds on the ground or around objects and white lights buzzing around individuals.

Belinda, a kind and caring young lady, found herself constantly attracting people who were bent on telling her their life story. These people were often complete strangers. Belinda had not knowingly encouraged this, but unconsciously she felt she had to save people. At times, this was overwhelming for her because she found it difficult to say no. It soon became a nuisance and distracted her from her spiritual development.

Healing The Need to Give Too Much

If, like Belinda, you are feeling drained by the demands of others, sit quietly and light a candle.

Write out the sentence "whatever I do is never enough because…" and write down all the answers that come into your mind until you run out. You may see pictures coming to mind of people you have been unable to please, or emotions rising through your body.

Think about Belinda's healing now. It will be easy for you to open the door to your own positive changes because of the healing she received. She has unlocked and prepared the psychic healing energies for you. Look deeply within yourself and find the part of you that doesn't feel you have done enough. Access the guilt. You could give the guilt a shape or a colour. You may see it as a guilty you or hear yourself being told that you are wrong.

Watch as this part of you heals and lets go of those guilty feelings. You may need to talk, cry or feel the inadequacy. Let the emotions and thoughts flow as the healing takes place.

Ask out loud that your powerful spiritual guardians come forward to support you. Let them take away and dissolve the feelings.

When you are healed, think about how you will know that you have done enough and that you are good enough to become an excellent psychic.

14

Where Does Psychic Energy Come From?

This chapter is very important. It is much easier to trust what is happening if you understand where your hunches or intuitive knowings come from. You will have an easier time convincing your logical mind if you trust the source of your intuitive flashes. You will know that if you seek advice, there is a world of difference between listening to a top professional with a clear track record as opposed to a novice whom you have never heard of. You will be naturally more receptive to the top professional. The same goes for a well-known make of shoes or a brand of food; we all trust reliable sources much more readily.

And it is the same when it comes to your mind. You will need to persuade your logical mind that it can trust so it feels comfortable with the changes that occur. For this to occur it will need some form of proof. Sarah was very lucky because she immediately had her proof without spending years looking for it. Janet felt the emotions associated with her husband's visits each night. She knew he was present because she could feel him just as if he were alive. So how are you going to prove to your mind that you are receiving a reliable source of information?

It is a good idea to begin by acquainting yourself with psychic energy. Some initial questions you might like to ask yourself are.

- Where do I think psychic knowledge comes from?
- Am I right to listen?
- Can I trust it?
- If not, why not?

Your Subconscious Mind

Psychic energy comes from different places. The first of these is your subconscious mind, which is like a huge reservoir of information. Everything is saved inside it. It automatically controls all of your daily functions, such as taking you to the loo, heating your body, keeping you breathing and pumping your heart. Everything that has ever happened to you is filed away and locked deep inside your subconscious. Under hypnosis, you would probably be able to access all of the things that had ever happened to you in this lifetime and any of your past lives. You would also be able to access your future because your subconscious does not understand time or space. It also does not understand what is real and what is not real and it does not have any reasoning powers. This is very useful because you could introduce ideas into it and if they are reinforced often enough, your subconscious will accept them as true. In hypnosis, you are able to change your subconscious thoughts rapidly.

In hypnosis, the conscious mind is kept happy and distracted while suggestions are purposefully dropped into the subconscious. Your subconscious is your real powerhouse. If it is not happy about a suggestion, or it has alternative information inside, such as "I will never make a good psychic" and you try to install new suggestions without eliminating that belief, it will instantly throw them out. This is why healing is so important.

The power of your subconscious is needed in order to receive psychic messages and translate them. It works in pictures and symbols. To develop clairvoyance you will need to be able to decipher the meanings of any images and symbols presented to you by your subconscious.

Hypnosis

Some years ago when I was hypnotised, I was taken back to when I was three years of age. I had dived headfirst from a chest of drawers into a cot and missed. I knocked out all of my baby front teeth on the top railing of the cot. I consciously remembered the incident. Even though before the hypnotic session I could have vaguely described it, under hypnosis I could remember minute details, such as the wooden cot rail, the small print on the lino floor and the exact shading of colours of that flooring. I could also recall all the colours and the design of the wallpaper in the bedroom. I could remember the length of time I was on the floor and the exact force at the moment of impact. I also remembered seeing my teeth on the floor with blood all around them and my mum's shocked reaction when she entered the room.

Psychic Flashes

When you daydream, ideas can suddenly pop into your mind from your subconscious. In this relaxed and receptive state, your subconscious can easily access its remarkable database and hey presto you will have a psychic flash. The trick is to realise that you have had a psychic flash or a sudden hunch. Practice using your subconscious more frequently and you will find that if you give it instructions it will obey.

- You need to tell it clearly what you want it to do.

- Begin by telling it to wake you up at a certain time of day.

- Ask it to remind you of something tomorrow.

- Ask it to bring back to mind something that happened to you at the age of seven that you have forgotten.

- Keep giving it instructions until you get results.

Auto Suggestion

Usually, speaking the command will not bring up an answer immediately, unless you instruct it to do so. You also need to get used to auto-suggestion; the art of telling yourself positive things. Some people call these statements affirmations. If you consistently show and tell your subconscious what you want, it will absorb the information and get on the case for you. Always give it very simple instructions and a bright, vivid picture to accompany the instructions. If you add feelings, your suggestion will go even deeper into your subconscious. NLP (Neuro Linguistic Programming) was created to teach athletes how to get the best out of themselves. Nowadays, it is used by millions of people who have learned how to improve their lives.

Your Subconscious Loves Pictures

Your mind loves pictures. Make them bright, clear and near to you and bring in lots of feelings, especially if you are an emotional person. If you want to be an effective psychic, a reputable healer and earning lots of money, see yourself giving people excellent readings. See your clients happy. Make the images colourful and bright, bring them closer in your mind's eye and enjoy the successful feelings in your body. Then say, "This or something even better is coming to me now." Talk in the present tense, because your subconscious does not understand the concept of a past or a future. It thinks everything is happening right now so it will not absorb any new ideas unless you talk to it in the present tense. Make friends with your subconscious and it will do you proud.

15

Telepathy

The second type of psychic experience is telepathy, mind-to-mind communication through psychic energy. This includes mind reading or ESP. It is the art of sending or receiving information to another's mind. A telepathic message can sometimes come out of the blue, or it can be deliberately sent. Spontaneous telepathy usually occurs when someone you know is in deep distress and sending out an SOS. You could also feel the intense impact of the state of their mind and emotions. Many people feel the death of a loved one in this way. They are able to sense the exact moment of parting, especially if that person is a member of the family. Premonitions also occur through telepathy. You may sense that someone you know is in danger or that something awful is about to happen. I sensed Princess Diana's death about eight weeks beforehand when I began dreaming of car accidents. I also started to meet more people than usual who were involved in car accidents.

Manifestation usually works through telepathy and there is great truth in the idea that like attracts like. How many times have you been thinking about someone, only to have them call you within minutes? Have you ever been seated or standing next to someone and felt really uncomfortable? If so then you are picking up on their thoughts. Mind reading occurs when you deliberately connect with another's mind. You can easily be trained to do this.

Have you ever begun to learn something new or wanted to buy a particular item and then noticed associated people, books or films popping up all over the place to help you? This is telepathy. Consciously or unconsciously you are sending messages and signals across the ethers to those who are on the same telepathic waveband. If you consciously focus on what you want and you believe you will draw it to you, it tends to happen faster. This is because you are using your entire mind potential – the mind energy of both your conscious and subconscious. This is the process of manifestation. Everything you could possibly wish for already exists. All you need to do is to draw it to you. Why not start to fine-tune your telepathic senses and your sixth sense and see what happens?

Unknowingly, you are telepathically tuning into many thousands of people at once without even realising it. I liken this level of communication through the Universal Mind to the adverts you see on television where beams of light shoot from one city and go all over the world. Television uses these types of images for advertising the news and telecommunications. I have also seen airlines advertising their flight routes in this way. The whole world transmits telepathically day and night, 24/7.

You Can Connect With Anyone

You have the ability to send your light beams all over the world and you can connect with anyone you wish. You only have to think of the recipient and the connection is made. The only thing that will stop you believing in this is your own lack of trust in the process.

Two of my young female friends were recently invited to go on Dragon's Den, the English TV programme where bright, innovative people are selected for investment into new business schemes. These two young ladies decided to send a few telepathic messages to the organisers of the programme. They then put together a video of their scheme, sent it in, did some more powerful mind work and thought no more of it. They knew their idea had been turbo charged into the ethers with enormous force. It was destined to manifest somewhere, hopefully in the minds of the people they wanted to telepathically contact.

The chances of appearing on this programme are rare and both girls had done their homework, really learning how to use their minds to the maximum effect to manifest it.

Sometimes, like these energetic young ladies, it is a good idea to send an idea with the maximum force and then let it go entirely. Place it entirely in God's hands. This is how magic works. Other times it is more effective to telepathically transport yourself into the minds of those you wish to respond to your ideas. Continue sending them telepathic messages and eventually they will respond. You can also place telepathic ideas and thoughts into people's minds to achieve a sense of calm. I have taught people how to overcome family squabbles in this way and bring the entire family back into a state of peace.

Psychic Clouds

According to our beliefs we group together with like-minded people to create and think in psychic blocks. For example, psychic students, healing groups, people who believe in angels, yoga practitioners, animal rights' groups, rebels and activists, all tend to gravitate towards one another inside their psychic energy group. A word of caution! It is important to ensure you are discerning about your thoughts to avoid attracting mass negative beliefs that could take over your mind.

When a drama occurs, for example 9/11, the pain and suffering of the thoughts of those involved caused a massive negative psychic cloud that hung over New York on the astral plane and weighed the New Yorkers down.

That psychic cloud not only still exists but sadly it has now grown much bigger as the incident infected many with intense fear. Each time you pass through security at an airport you are unwillingly buying into that collective fear and increasing the size of that psychic cloud. You can refuse to participate by protecting your thoughts, reassuring yourself that you are perfectly safe at all times. You can ask that any past effects are washed out of your aura. You can also serve Spirit by asking that healing and love is sent to the astral plane to disperse the negative psychic cloud. This is the way forward.

During the World Cup or any big sporting event, if a country loses, a negative psychic cloud is created, which absorbs all the frustration and heartbreak of the thousands of affected fans. Because of the immense power of television and the vast numbers of people involved, it has a huge impact on the psychic airwaves. The disappointment is then analysed and discussed for years, adding greatly to the size of the cloud and its power. I often wonder how the poor football player unfortunate enough to have lost the goal copes with the intense level of psychic attack directed towards him. Negative psychic clouds of energy can draw you in, so be vigilant in your thinking and try not to get involved.

16

The Super Conscious Realms

Psychic energy also comes from the higher super conscious planes. We all have access to a Higher Source of Love and knowing, the place where inspirations, breakthroughs, warnings, urges and understandings come from. I know when I am working in the super conscious as I have to direct my psychic perception out further. My psychic antennae pick up an energy all around my head and it can feel like I am leaving and going space travelling. I step into my super conscious mind and at that point I know I am in another dimension. While there, I may have to wait to be shown what to do next. It is a bit like being a radar transmitter.

In this state it is uncomfortable if someone talks and tries to engage me in a conversation. If you are psychically bringing information through from the super conscious realms, you will be able to talk to whoever you are giving a reading to, but you may not be able to listen to their words as it will interrupt your flow. You are too busy receiving images and messages from somewhere that can seem quite far away and this requires concentration and quiet. The impressions coming from the higher realms can be very subtle. Angels can be clairvoyantly seen from here as well as high spiritual guardians, custodians of light, deities, Gods and Goddesses.

When I receive messages from a relative who has passed on, they are generally denser and nearer the person in front of me having the reading. I can usually see the deceased, feel them, hear them talking to me, or all three. They are nearby, occupying space in the room. They are touching the person they have left behind or standing very close to them. I am always surprised when the loved one cannot feel them or see them because they are so clear to me. When doing distant healing for someone living in another country, a similar thing occurs and I know I am telepathically picking up information about them as well as healing. I can see them in the same way as if they are in the room with me. Remember, psychic energy does not recognise time or space.

Distance Healing

I once taught a group of psychic healing students to use crystal dowses (pendulums) to heal. They were beginners and they had very little healing experience. We did some distance healing for a lady in New Zealand and because of the time difference between England and New Zealand, I saw her asleep in bed. I then felt something I had never witnessed before; the whole group was transported over to her on the ethers to enact a healing. We all hovered above her bed and everyone involved was aware of this. We stayed until she had received enough energy and until our crystals had stopped spinning. The crystal pendulums were collecting cosmic energy from the super conscious realms and redirecting it straight into the etheric body of the lady, which was physically charged with high potency energy. Three hours later, her daughter rang me from New Zealand to say that her mother had broken out in a hot sweat and was delirious during the time of the healing. The girl had been very frightened and thought her mother would die. Amazed, she told me that the fever had finally worn off and her mother had woken and was now feeling much better.

The students felt elated and they were very proud of their achievement. They had not known the lady's name so they received proof that they were developing the ability to psychically heal someone. I had only told them the daughter's first name and I asked them to link into her mother's energy.

Angels Live in the Super Consciousness

If a deceased relative needs healing or a message is relayed from one dead spirit to another dead spirit and then passed on to me, the dead spirits seem just a bit further away from Earth. Unless there is a high guide involved, it all takes place on the lower astral planes of consciousness. However, if a deep healing takes place and I ask for the help of the angels or ascended masters, my energy changes subtly. I move into my super conscious mind and the realms of the super conscious, where it all becomes wider, vaster and lighter. The super conscious is lighter and much more beautiful. It contains your conscious mind and your subconscious mind, as well as the collective consciousness of the world's entire population. The super conscious is the realm of the Divine, the Angels, the Elohim (creator gods), the extraterrestrials, the Galactic Council, the Spiritual Guides and the Spiritual Guardians.

Your Super Conscious Mind

You have the ability to tune in and harmonise with your super conscious mind and in doing this you will have a much deeper than average appreciation and a heightened ability to attract what you want.

The super conscious is limitless or infinite in nature. It contains God, Brahman, Supreme Energy, Source, Universe, Universal Intelligence, Higher Power and such like.

Your super conscious mind exists as an infinite field of potential, which knows no boundaries or limitations and it is all encompassing. It is within everything and it exists everywhere.

Within this Infinite Field of Potential is anything that has ever happened or been created in the past, everything which is currently being created, or whatever may be created in the future. The super conscious mind contains every conceivable emotion, such as love, joy, peace, patience, kindness, goodness, faithfulness, gentleness and self-control, along with fear, doubt, worry, sadness, turmoil, anger and greed. Whichever of these you choose to think about will eventually come to pass in your life. Having said that, it is not a good idea to worry about this, especially if you are going through a tough time and you need to release the negative thoughts. Keep an open countenance and observe that negativity is there. Whatever you do, do not suppress it, just heal the thoughts as soon as you can. Too many people worry about the outcome of their thoughts when negative emotions are natural and serve to try and heal you.

The super conscious mind also consists of you, your family, your neighbours, your friends and your work colleagues. It is necessary for you to realise that when broken down into its purest form, everything seen or unseen is made of pure energy or light. This light consists of a vibrating mass of energy, which makes up every possible outcome. That is why accessing the light is so important for your evolution.

Use Your Imagination

Your ability to imagine is a powerful step to developing psychically. Imagine that you can sense the differences, as I do, with the three sources of psychic energy: your subconscious mind, telepathy and your super conscious mind. Imagine that you are now receptive to receiving and relaying psychic information; that you are a psychic transmitter. The psychic information comes to you like a wave, then it passes through you into your thoughts before being translated into speech. Finally it pours out through your voice. Imagine you know which spiritual plane it has come from; either the lower planes, telepathy, spirit or Divine beings of Light on the beautiful and higher super conscious planes of existence.

17

Your Higher Self

Just above your head, living in the higher beautiful realms of the super conscious, is your Higher Self; a magnificent, radiant, growing life-force. I usually see someone's Higher Self as a wonderful pale golden energy around the top of their head and stretching above them. To mediums or psychics who are constantly drawing energy down from their higher selves to help others, these energies may appear as shimmering lights. The lights pour down into the medium's aura through the crown chakra. I once saw a photo of a medium giving healing. A brilliant light was almost covering his entire face and head. It was very beautiful.

For people who are not yet spiritually awake or who are unaware of their higher selves, it may float as high as fifty feet above their head. Unfortunately, for these unawakened souls, the power of their Higher Self is less radiant and less available to them. Nevertheless, it is always present and subtly directing their soul.

Your Higher Self is a very loving and very kind energy and it knows what difficulties and challenges you have brought to Earth with you to overcome. It supports you with those challenges, but it cannot remove them for you. It accompanies you through each of your lifetimes and goes with you into death and new births.

Your Higher Self holds all the memories and knowledge of each of your former lifetimes and it always wants to help you grow. Your everyday consciousness is an aspect of your Higher Self that lives in your physical world. Contained within the energy of your Higher Self are all the memories and knowledge of your former lifetimes or previous experiences, as well as your future. It is a very wise teacher indeed. It communicates with

you through your intuition, coincidences and synchronisation –
by way of people, books, films and any other way it can to pass
messages to you. It is completely limitless and totally unattached
to your desire. That is why I say it cannot take away your
challenges for you, or else you would not grow.

*I once remember a young man who had money issues
and was crying out to his Higher Self for help. He was
desperate and very frightened and he wanted his Higher
Self to take his problem away. For years he had not
listened to advice and he had squandered his money.
He had also been a petty thief. Within hours of begging
his Higher Self for help, someone stole his wallet and he
lost even more money. Disillusioned, he called me and
told me that asking his Higher Self for help had not
worked. In fact, it had made the problem worse.*

*I asked Spirit what was happening and I was told
that the money problems were old karma that needed
to be redressed. It was necessary for him to learn to
save money and respect it more readily. He was also
being asked to face up to his problems. Like many of
us, he unconsciously wanted to remain as a child and
have someone look after him. He put the phone down
not only disgruntled with me, but also disappointed with
his Higher Self. He was not ready to heed the message
and he did not understand the role of his Higher Self.
Perhaps, if he had asked his Higher Self to show him
how to gain the necessary courage to face his
challenges and find a way to replace what he had
stolen from others, the response might have been very
different. Who knows?*

Linking in to Your Higher Self

Once you increase your awareness of your Higher Self, you will greatly enhance your spiritual and psychic progress. It will always guide you. You will take an enormous leap forward in your spiritual growth by simply talking to it daily.

You can also ask your Higher Self to talk to another's Higher Self and reach a peaceful conclusion if you have been having difficulties. This always works if you are truly ready to forgive yourself and them. You can also request your Higher Self to do this on your behalf so you know what grievances or resentments you carry towards that person. Powerful healings are enacted in this way.

Universal Law

The resolution to your concern may not unfold in the way you expect because you are working with universal law. Universal law is detached and impartial and it looks for the most convenient way to resolve issues, not necessarily those which are most comfortable for you. The universe has many more strings to its bow than we do and it often brings us a resolution in a unique way. If you want to work with your Higher Self in this way, be open to accept whatever it decides to do. You can also ask your Higher Self for a symbol, a picture or a message about how ready to grow you are, or someone else is and how much assistance you should be giving them. In fact you can ask for practically anything you like. If you do not receive a response, look at your reaction within and clear this. Everything has meaning, even the lack of response. Remember the man with the money issue was just asking the wrong questions.

Take a moment right now to imagine how your Higher Self looks to you. You might picture it as a beautiful radiant light, completely surrounding you with its love. Later on, I demonstrate the enormous power of the Higher Self when Graham, a clairsentient (sense-orientated) student wanted proof of its spiritual existence.

18

Spirit Guides

Spirit guides, like us humans, come in all shapes and sizes and from many different backgrounds. You might have a deceased granny watching over you, or a wise archetype from a Native American tribe. As I mentioned earlier, my first encounter was a Chinese guide who called herself Chinese Woman and was thousands of years old. Your spirit guides might come from countries like Egypt and they may have a past life connection with you. You may have known each other many times before. Perhaps you have reincarnated while they prefer to remain in Spirit. I have also met people with Romany gypsies as guides, who have gypsies way back in their family tree.

Think about your own guides for a moment. As you do so you might feel that they have never been human, or you may get a sense that they know our Earth very well and have had many lives here. A number of different spirit guides will come and go as you grow and evolve. They change as you do.

Your Guardian Angel

You also have many angels guiding you. Angel guides may hold vows you have put in place in your past. They are not allowed to put down their responsibility until instructed by you to do so. This happens when you realise you have these vows and you choose to dissolve them. Each of us also has an angelic guide who is our guardian angel. Your guardian angel is with you from the moment of your conception and it is by your side at your birth. At death your guardian angel holds you lovingly and transports you to the inner planes. Spirit teacher guides step in when you are learning something new and stay with you until you perfect it. Whether you believe in spirit guides or not, whether you can see, hear or sense them, if you are to progress as a medium, psychic, clairvoyant or healer, spirit guides will form a vital part of your work.

Invisible Friends

Do you remember having an invisible friend when you were a child? If so, you may not have realised that this friend could have been a spirit guide. Some of the guides who work with you as a child will have moved on when you reached a certain age. My sister and I had invisible horses, which were invisibly tied to the car by an invisible rope. As we drove out on Sunday afternoons to play in the forest, if Dad drove the car too quickly, we would grow quite upset worrying that our horses could not keep up the pace. To us they were absolutely real! I spent hours at the bottom of the garden speaking to invisible elves and fairies. If you have never had an invisible friend and if you have not seen or felt the existence of spirit guides or angels, it might help to imagine a higher form of entity surrounding you as a focal point for any potential messages or healing you receive or pass to others. I talk out loud to my guides and it works. They do not always talk back but they impress information onto me through impulses or knowings. The impressions can be very subtle, so do not expect a booming great voice to fill your head.

A Mighty Presence

Nevertheless, there is always the exception to any rule. A lady called Shirley came to see me recently. She was going through a bad break-up of her marriage. Her husband had discovered Viagra and run off with a much younger woman. He was being hateful to his wife and, as she worked with him on a professional basis, it was increasingly difficult for her to go to the office. I could clearly see that she felt very wronged and she wanted to get even. She wanted him to hurt as much as she did.

During her reading, a large number of spirits suddenly emerged. The energy was huge and they were transmitting a very strong message from her soul to relinquish her feelings of revenge. They told me she had chosen, on the inner planes, to move on from him. Their karma was over and they were going on to lead very different lives. She was experiencing a great resistance to letting go and the voices around me gathered pace and became insistent and extremely urgent. I asked her to let go again as her guides entered into her aura and a mighty pressure built up around her head.

Shirley finally agreed as the pressure was unbearable. The moment she agreed, the guides stepped up the power, forced the negativity out of her and healed her. She burst into tears and all the hurt and dark years of bitterness poured out of her heart. As she cried, the pressure in her head subsided. I was told by her spirit guides that her life would now turn around for the better. Shirley had been locked up in a power struggle that had no useful conclusion. The guides told me that had she continued, she would have spent thousands of pounds on a court case. The fight in the court would have gone on for years culminating in a stroke for him and a heart attack for her.

Native American Guides and Animal Guides

If you have been Native American in a former life, identifying your totem or power creature will feel right as this was one of the first initiation rights for men and women. You may be drawn to shamanic practices and animal guides. I have met many psychics who have Native American chiefs as spirit guides. I have also worked with animals in Spirit, who are still protecting their owners. Stop for a moment and get a sense of whether or not you feel this type of guide feels right for you.

Linked to native shamanism are the Pleiadians who are multi-dimensional spirit beings from Pleiades. Pleiades is a cluster of beautiful, dazzling stars located in the constellation of Taurus. The Pleiadians are here to assist you with your process of spiritual transformation. They are highly evolved light beings and they are the next step on your human evolution. They reside at a very high frequency that is much lighter than we know.

Indian Deities

In India, spirituality and religion are a part of everyday life. In no other country will you see a renounced ascetic with only a blanket and rosary as his possessions without attracting attention. India is home to spirituality and all the major religions of the world that have been thriving in harmony for many centuries.

The Indian Gods, Goddesses and Deities (supernatural immortal beings) will appeal to you if you have had past lives as an Indian. If this is the case, you could find yourself attending spiritual meetings where you chant mantras as this will align you with the energy of the deity. It is a profound process of spiritual purification. For help, call upon Lord Brahma, the creator of the universe to uplift and purify your mind; Lord Vishnu, the preserver of the world to re-establish balance between good and evil; Lord Shiva for help with endings and new cycles; Lord

Ganesha to eradicate obstacles; Lord Krishna to destroy all your pain; and Lord Rama, the embodiment of truth and reality for impeccability. Call upon Lakshmi, the female Divine Consort of Lord Vishnu for wealth and good fortune; Kali, sometimes called the Goddess of Death for destruction of demons and the death of your ego; and Saraswati, the feminine Divine Consort of Lord Brahma for knowledge and wisdom.

Gods and Goddesses

Gods and Goddesses are playing a vital role in the evolution of our planet. Throughout time, the Virgin Mary and Mother Earth (the guardian owl in the great tree of the world) have been custodians of the feminine goddess energy. The Star Goddess (she is the dust whose feet are the hosts of heaven and whose body encircles the whole universe) is overseeing the beginning and ending of your sacred journey. Over time many other Goddesses have been called forth to help, including Isis, the Egyptian Goddess of magic; Artemis, Goddess of the Light and protector of the vulnerable; Astarte, Goddess of fertility; Diana, the Roman Goddess of the moon; and Melusine, the serpent Goddess.

You may feel drawn to the Greek, Egyptian or Chinese Gods and Goddesses for guidance. If you align with Egypt – and many psychics do – call upon Isis, the Egyptian Goddess of magic to help you with Divine magic and feminine power. To help you develop psychically you will find it especially helpful to call upon Gods and Ascended Masters such as Apollo, the Greek Sun God who oversees prophecy; Merlin, the great old sage-wizard; Thoth, the Egyptian God of high magic, symbols, and astronomy; and Master St Germain, the Wonderman of Europe. Kuan Ti, the Chinese Warrior God who acts to prevent war, is a prophet who predicts the future. Call upon Kuan Ti and he will protect you from the lower spirits.

Alien Guides

Begin to live in your heart. Do nice things for others that help them and at the same time do nice things for yourself. This opens up the compassion within you. When you open your heart, it is easier to make a closer connection with your spirit guides. Heart people are more aware of guides than head people. If you are a head person your spirit guides could be more alien in nature according to where they have originated from. If you have always believed in, and had a strong interest in ETs (Extra Terrestrials) or UFOs (Unidentified Flying Objects) and you sense that you come from another galaxy, you could be from the star Sirius or one of the other star clusters or planets. Your guides will be unemotional and very matter-of-fact. They are usually highly practical, knowledgeable and very advanced.

There are many levels of guides in the spirit world. Each guide is different and you will be attracted to exactly the right guide who is in tune with your frequency. This rich world of spirit is virtually unknown to most people, but if you do not let the limitations of your logical mind hold you back, your spirit guide will find you and show you the way.

The spirit world is as highly populated as ours so a great deal of guidance is available. There are guides who are your deceased family members; guides you have known in your past lives and guides who are here to teach you. There are also healer guides who can help you become physically and emotional stronger. Around you there are nature spirits that live amongst the trees and fields, animal spirits and happy guides to lift your mood. There are angels, archangels, saints, devas, aliens, masters and God, the Creator of all.

I want you to know what I know so that you can be blessed by the support of your guides. If you do not know about all of this help and support available, you are missing out. When you connect with your spirit and angelic guides, your life will become easier. Unlock your heart and be wide open to the existence of all these wonderful beings of Light and Love who are here to help you.

To connect with your guides you will need to notice subtle clues. Raise your awareness enough to notice guidance, input, or help when it is being offered. Being able to accept help can prove difficult as most of us have been conditioned to expect difficulties. We have been conditioned to put ourselves down and call ourselves "selfish" if we take too much time out for ourselves or if we ask too much of another. You may need to break this conditioning down because you need time in order to develop properly.

Nature Spirits

Many years ago I attended an energy workshop in Wales. We all went for a summer afternoon's walk into the woods when I suddenly saw tree spirits clearly visible inside the trunks of trees. This was a first for me and it did not happen again for many years. That day I discovered that if I stood inside the aura of a person who was able to clairvoyantly see nature spirits, I could do the same. The spiritual teacher taking the workshop worked extensively with nature spirits. He lived in the countryside with them all around him and he spent many hours in the forests and woods. On another occasion I witnessed lots of tiny fairies jumping over my feet whilst I was explaining to a group of people how to communicate with nature spirits. Several other very surprised people witnessed this beautiful spectacle at the same time. The fairies wore all different shades of blue and they were about eighteen inches high. It was a magical moment.

Nature is inhabited by thousands of different creatures of all kinds. Their energy is often subtle and so they are not always easy to identify. Some of them take care of the plants and animals, while others are responsible for the trees and stones.

Incarnated Elementals

If you look at some people you will see that they seem to carry the energy of the elementals. This is because they are incarnated elementals. Their physical features look like fairies, elves, pixies, gnomes, leprechauns, mermaids, dolphins, incarnated animals, or unicorns. If you think you might be an incarnated elemental, you would be a fun-loving individual, possibly enjoying a practical joke and a good laugh. Elementals can be mischievous and they have a long history with wizards, witches and sorceresses. In the spiritual elemental kingdom the fairies, elves and the others hold parties filled with laughter and storytelling.

A few weeks ago I was seated in a pub at a table full of actors, professional entertainers and musicians. I became aware of just how light these people were and I thought they were all elementals. One even looked like a leprechaun. I was astonished when I mentioned this to a girl who had fairy wings attached to her dress. She listened and then confirmed this to me as if it were an everyday occurence. It was totally acceptable and normal for her.

Elementals prefer the company of animals or plants to that of humans. If you are an incarnated elemental you may have fairies, elves or leprechauns with you as spirit guides. They are very helpful and you can call upon them at any time. The happiest incarnated Earth elementals are outside in nature walking their dogs.

Nature spirits are happy to be given spiritual work to do. Try to make contact with them and communicate with them. Admire the lovely work they do as this will fill them with joy. You can also ask all of these beautiful creatures to collaborate in Divine work for humanity. The next time you go for a walk in the woods, try speaking to all the little creatures and ask them to reveal themselves to you.

Recognise That You Are a Spirit

As soon as you realise that you are a spirit as well as a physical body, it becomes easier to connect with those in the invisible world. Begin to talk to your own spirit more readily. You could begin by asking it a few simple questions. Ask it, "What does my spirit want to do today that would make it happy" "What does my spirit say about this situation?" "What does my spirit think about this person?" Have conversations with your spirit and find out its needs. It might like retail therapy, it may like quiet places in the sun, it may love swimming or riding a bike, or being with lots of people, dancing, listening to the radio, watching television, or having a quiet cup of coffee. Notice what it likes to eat. Notice what lifts and inspires you. When do you feel at your most confident? When do you lose yourself in a task? Notice what inspires your spirit.

Connecting with your spirit will make connecting with your spirit guides far easier. When you have connected with your own spirit, begin to notice what other people's spirits are like and what makes them tick. Try your best friends first, then family members and perhaps work colleagues. Someone's spirit lies dormant under their personality and you may be surprised to get a quite different feedback when you do this exercise. I recently did this with a difficult lady and found her spirit to be very loving. See if you can feel the spirit of any animals you know. If you get stuck in your head or feel disconnected from your heart centre, this could feel a little strange to begin with. If this happens, open your heart and sense another's spirit in just one word, like "reliable," "steady," "warm," "cold," "dull," "bright," "young," "heavy," "quick," "wise" or "old."

When I did this, I discovered that my spirit is very young and it loves to eat sweets. Before this, I had an older personality inside my head, which told me off for eating sweets. I dissolved the guilt that had occurred from listening to too many people telling me that it is not good to eat sugar. Now I eat as many sweets as I want because I know I love them. Sweets lift my spirit. When I eat sweets my spirit is full of glee and I feel young and happy.

Now you understand this, spend some time getting to know what your spirit would love to have to make it feel more carefree. You may have spent very little time giving your spirit what it needs to feel cared for and nourished. Find out and you will feel so much better and more alive.

19

The Angels

When I began to work spiritually, I worked extensively with spirit guides and I did not have a great deal to do with angels. Many of my spiritual colleagues connected to them, but for years I felt nothing. I remember drawing and painting pictures of angels when I was a child and I used to love the idea of someone having a golden halo around their head. I particularly loved the picture of Jesus with a golden halo talking to young children who also had golden haloes. I then forgot all about them.

As I have evolved I have come to notice angels and their existence in many of my readings as they subtly began to appear. I do not remember the exact moment this occurred, but it must have been very natural because I was so laid back about it all. I also noticed that a lot of good things were happening to people in need who believed in angels. Their prayers were heard and suddenly someone or something would turn up to help them. After the event, when they tried to find that person to thank them, no one seemed to know who there were. Stories like this are very common in maternity wards and hospices.

During workshops I have encountered huge angels with a massive wing span. I have also seen them hover behind someone when a deep healing is taking place. They bring an immense sense of peace and grace, which completely fills the room. This grace can feel like the Holy Spirit has descended and engulfed everyone. It is always accompanied by a deep and silent peace.

Diana's Miraculous Transformation

Diana, an outgoing red-haired English woman, enrolled on one of my psychic development workshops. When I asked her how long she thought it would take her to develop she told me five years. I intuitively knew otherwise, but I did not say anything because the time was not right. Later that day, we were learning to see auras. When it came to Diana's turn to have her aura read by the class, a massive angel descended. Diana's spirit was gently lifted out of her body and placed slightly above her left hand side. Her floating spirit was safely suspended in the ethers. Etheric connections were then made to lift her etheric body energy higher in order to align her for the psychic work ahead. For twenty minutes her physical body was completely ashen and grey. For those in the room who could see clairvoyantly, it was an awe-inspiring experience. For those who could not, the physical changes that occurred fascinated them. It was essential that she was not touched at this time and that the class did not panic.

Diana's spirit then floated gently back into her physical form. She was quite shaken up and she didn't know where she was. It was also unclear who or what had completed the spiritual changes, for the only spiritual phenomenon we could see was the mighty angel. When I asked the angel about this, I was shown almost imperceptible energies moving and changing her state like tiny waves. I believe there were many thousands of changes made to her meridians and psychic cells. When she returned to her body, she needed to sit in silence for a while. We wrapped her up, made her a warm cup of tea and she ate a banana. Her body temperature was icy.

Less than an hour later, Diana was able to bring through psychic messages with complete ease. What she had thought would take five years had just taken twenty *minutes. The angel was huge, beautiful, softly coloured and appeared to be male.*

A Deep Healing by Archangel Mary, Queen of the Angels

On another occasion when a deep healing was taking place in Northern Ireland, I saw Archangel Mary, Queen of the Angels and Mother of Christ surrounded by a host of beautiful descending angels. The room lit up and we could all feel her Divine presence. It was everywhere. No one spoke, but each lady came forward and gently touched another lady shedding silent tears until everyone in the room was standing. Every single woman in the room had lost a baby, many through abortion, which was a subject not spoken about during that time in Ireland. Two minutes before, I had no idea of these losses, but I intuitively knew that the healing had to be conducted in silence. I also had no idea until that very moment that Archangel Mary was responsible for the healing of mothers and children.

Angels Are Different From Spirit Guides

For me, experiencing the difference between spirit guides and angels was quite an eye opener. Spirit guides can look and feel denser than angels. They have lived at least one lifetime here on Earth, so they are able to relate to your physical challenges. The angels have a more subtle, lighter energy and they sometimes come forward surrounded by shimmering lights and incredible colours which are unseen by the physical eye. The colours are lighter and more translucent than the colours we see here on Earth. I have been completely bowled over by the size of some of these angels, as many of them are enormous. They have never lived here and they have no free will like we humans do. They are lighter than us because they are closer to God. Their duty is to serve us and they act as Divine messengers from God.

On one occasion, when the psychic energy in my house was heavy and dense, a friendly medium told me to call in the angels of the air, which clean spiritual atmospheres. He told me to open all the windows wide. I am ashamed to admit that as I opened the windows, I did not feel convinced that it would work. Imagine my astonishment when I suddenly saw a whole host of tiny golden cherubs with minute golden dustpans and brushes fly in through the windows. The golden cherubs rapidly cleaned the air and lifted the atmosphere with their little golden brushes. They flew out as quickly as they had flown in. The room smelled of a beautiful light fragrance and it was full of shimmering golden light.

Angels have a much higher vibration than most guides since they are so close to God. They will protect, inspire, energise and empower you and they may even influence you through your conscience. Unlike your guides, they will not offer you advice, but they offer support instead. One student of mine constantly spoke to the angels expecting them to answer him back. I told him, "It is your spiritual guides who are better equipped to do this." With practice, you will get an increased sense of angels and notice things that help you. Angels work through subtle guidance. Things will happen if you are intuitively alert and you will be able to match synchronisations and coincidences to requests you have made. Angels play a majorly significant role in healing.

20

The Archangels

You have a guardian angel who has been by your side throughout all of your births and will remain with you for eternity. There are also archangels who are usually concerned with global issues. Seven of these archangels are well known for their direct help with humanity. They are Archangel Michael, Archangel Jophiel, Archangel Chamuel, Archangel Gabriel, Archangel Raphael, Archangel Uriel and Archangel Zadkiel. You can approach these powerful archangels directly whenever you need their particular area of expertise.

You can call upon the archangels for the following help:

Archangel Michael for courage

Archangel Jophiel for inspiration

Archangel Chamel for organisation and grief

Archangel Gabriel to reach your highest potential

Archangel Raphael for healing

Archangel Uriel for problem-solving

Archangel Zadkiel for forgiveness.

The Archangels and Healing

When working psychically, you need to be able to ask for healing for your client. It is always a safe bet to call upon the angels and it is a good idea to know who to ask.

The archangels are linked to healing so when you have learned to channel and you can psychically pick up imbalances and disease in others, ask them to come through and heal that person. Archangel Raphael is a powerful archangel responsible for healing, abundance, creativity, truth and vision. His twin flame is Mary, mother of Jesus. Mary is the queen of the angels.

These angels help doctors, nurses, healers and mothers. If you wish to open your third eye and develop psychic vision, Archangel Raphael can help you. He is the patron saint of the blind. Raphael also assists in improving your concentration and focus. He can direct powerful healing power into your heart to remove disease and bring in love to enable your heart to be healthy.

Cutting the Psychic Cords

Archangel Michael is the warrior angel who stands for courage. He will bring you courage and willpower and free you from fear. Archangel Michael is often called upon to cut the cords with those you have problems or dilemmas with. That is not to say that the people from whom you are cutting the ties will necessarily leave your life. It is more to do with cleansing and clearing the adverse history and energies between you so that you have a clean slate to go on. Michael protects and he has a host of mighty angels working with him. He wears a deep blue cloak of protection that you can ask him to put around you. You can also make sure others are protected by asking Archangel Michael to wrap his deep blue cloak safely around them too. An archangel's influence is very powerful indeed; it is quite possible for them to save someone's life. Psychically protect your home, your possessions and your loved ones with the incredible might of this powerful archangel.

A Psychic Brainwave

I am particularly linked to Archangel Jophiel whom I have seen on a number of occasions when I need inspiration. Archangel Jophiel is the angel of wisdom and illumination. His twin flame is Christine and together they light up humanity. They discharge vast forces of light to dissolve negativity. These light currents flow around your brain. Whenever you get a sudden brainwave, after having tried to unravel a problem, Archangel Jophiel will be there to bring you the solution. Archangel Jophiel is the Patron of Artists and the archangel associated with art and beauty.

Archangel Chamuel and his twin flame Charity will encourage you to be more organised and clear-headed. Pray to Chamuel if someone you are reading for has lost a loved one and their heart is breaking. If they cannot forgive that person, Chamuel and Charity will help them to open their heart and let go of any emotional blockages. Archangel Chamuel rules the angels of love and you can ask for these angels to help you find things you have lost. You can also ask these angels to engulf you in love.

Archangel Gabriel and his twin flame Hope will help you to achieve your highest potential. They are able to show you what you have agreed to do on Earth and they can guide you towards the right people. If you need clarity or discipline, Gabriel will help you by aiding your ascension pathway and enabling you to absorb more light. He always attends the birth of a child, overseeing the arrival of the new soul.

Archangel Uriel is the great archangel who commands the angels of peace. His twin flame is Aurora and they work on transformation and forgiveness. You can ask Archangel Uriel for guidance when you do not understand another's motives or a hidden agenda. Uriel with Jesus Christ teaches selfless service and promotes closeness. Archangel Uriel is considered to be one of the wisest of the archangels. This archangel will help you with Divine magic, the dissolution of fear in the solar plexus, the development of your solar plexus and your soul's wisdom.

The Peace Angels

Archangel Uriel governs the peace angels; beautiful beings of light. If they come to you, you will feel a sense of deep peace and stillness. They may ask you to make a haven of peace in your home or town. This will be somewhere you can go to be at peace with yourself. It does not have to be a large space. In fact it can be something as simple as a special chair. Do not enter this place unless you feel entirely peaceful, for if you do you will rock its peaceful vibrations. If you enter the space peacefully you will then see the vibrations increase in this area of your home. Be sure to let peaceful thoughts flow through your mind whenever you think about this place.

Archangel Zadkiel and his twin flame Amethyst, bring forgiveness, compassion and mercy. He will encourage you to free yourself from your negativity and any limitations. If you are willing to forgive yourself or another then Archangels Zadkiel and Amethyst will release the karma between you. He will also help you to become more diplomatic when difficulties arise. Archangel Zadkiel worked with Saint Germain to bring us the Violet Flame, which is powerful enough to heal anything.

Children Can See Angels

Before they go to school and enter the busy world of education, children can see and talk with angels. This is because their right brain is open to such experiences. When your right brain is developed, you are more intuitive, psychic and imaginative. Education leans heavily towards left brain activity with its emphasis on competition, success and maths. If you can remember seeing angels as a child, go back into your past and fantasise again. You will return in the perfect mood to reconnect with your angels and enjoy their wonderful love.

21

The Lords of Karma

There are also angels that are of an even higher ranking and far more powerful than the archangels. These great angels are called the Lords of Karma. There are seven of them and they sit on a karmic board. They are responsible for keeping the records of humanity, called the Akashic Records. Everything about you is noted in these records which are stored on the ethereal planes. For a long time I thought the board of the Lords of Karma was a stern angelic council where all our past actions had to be brought to justice. I then realised that most of the Lords of Karma are goddesses and they are very compassionate. They reside over the Akashic Records of all humanity keeping a diary of your karma. Karma is the just return of everything you have sent out. There are seven high angels on the board, The Great Divine Director, The Goddess of Liberty, Lady Nada, Pallas Athena (Goddess of Truth), Elohim Vista, Kwan Yin (Goddess of Mercy) and Lady Portia, the spokesperson for the Karmic Board and Goddess of Justice. Each of these angels has fulfilled their Divine plan whilst here on Earth and they serve as teachers of mankind.

Your Karma Can Be Cancelled

You may not realise it, but your karma, the outcome of your past experiences and the future of your destiny, can be cancelled if your request is truly sincere. It may already have been cancelled without your awareness as the Earth's consciousness is rising so quickly now. For this to occur you can go before the Board and ask that your karma be dissolved. There are specially worded invocations for this. If you have misused your psychic power in a past life and you somehow "know" this, it might be a good idea to invoke the Lords of Karma and place your case in front of them. Sometimes, however, it is deemed appropriate for your soul to go through a particular karmic experience to learn and grow. Karma protects us, for without it those who have committed crimes with no remorse whatsoever would continue to do so.

The Akashic Records

The Akashic Records are said to be the knowledge of everything that has ever existed. They are not found in our physical world but reside in the ethers from the God Government up to the highest octaves upon the Etheric Plane, beyond the frequency of Fire. At the highest of Etheric Retreats lies the Temple Immaculate and an enormous Blue Flame of Sacred Fire. This retreat is where all life's records are stored, as well the libraries of genetic encodements for the whole of humanity. Every Gift, every Talent, and all Knowledge is etched in the Book of Wisdom that represents the Book of Life. This means that all knowledge about every human being, animal, plant or mineral is encoded within these timeless records.

Akasha is a Sanskrit word which means "space." It is said that Ancient civilisations, such as the Indians, Moors, Tibetans, Persians, Greeks, Chinese, Hebrews, Christians, Druids and Mayans have all claimed access to the Akasha.

Nostradamus is also said to have gained access to the Akasha and he has been proved to be highly accurate in his predictions even after many hundreds of years. It is also claimed that the wise mystics who could read the Akashic Records were highly revered and were invited to read for the Egyptian Pharaohs on everyday matters and dream interpretation. The Bible refers to the Akasha Records as the "Book of Life."

It is said that we all contribute to the Akashic Records, which contain all events; past, present and future. When accessing your future, the events are already known, but how you react to that future is not. The Akashic reader can tell you your future based on how you have responded in the past. If, however, you react differently now, you will change that prediction because you have free will and nothing is written in stone.

The Akasha is that magical substance otherwise known as the Philosopher's Stone from which the natural principles of Earth, air, fire and water are made up.

Gaining Access to the Akashic Records

Most people do not believe they can gain access to the Akashic Records, but I have seen them on numerous occasions. The first time I was not particularly looking or asking to view the Akashic Records and the psychic impressions came pouring through. The records reside in the ethers so the information comes through impressions that are unformed and which convert into pictures, words, or senses as they approach our Earth plane. Remember this is etheric energy so you would need to lighten and convert your energy to ether and float with the ethers if you were ever to journey to them.

It is possible for you to go and look at your records during a spiritually-guided meditation, but you may have to adjust your vibration to read them. It is also possible to look at another's records, but you will not be given access if it is deemed inappropriate. You can find out why you are here, why you know the people you do and the spiritual contracts between you. Accessing the records will help you to unwind events that may have puzzled you about your life.

Destiny Versus Reality

We now come to the question of how much of your life has been planned and how much control you have over your future? As a potential psychic or medium this will have deeper connotations because you will be dealing with other people's possible futures. Having given thousands of readings and worked closely with astrologers and numerologists for many years, I believe that each of us has chosen a definite life plan, which has been agreed with the Karmic Lords before our arrival here. For some people that plan is quite precise and for others it is more loosely woven.

When the Time is Right

This has recently been confirmed in a reading I gave to a single lady in her fifties who was about to enter a relationship with a man from the Arab emirates. To be with this man, she would have to uproot from her home in southern Spain and leave her financial independence behind.

She was ready to hear this information and she had been communicating via Skype with a gentleman, many years her junior, for some weeks. In her heart she knew he was "the one" despite the fact that others did not and warned her off him. He was attentive, interested in her, consistent in his approach and he communicated regularly. He texted her, called her and sent her flowers.

Her last love interest had been Swedish and a cool, distant character. Her tendency had been to attract men who always had a woman in the background – sometimes their mother who was overly jealous or protective. The lady in question had done the psychic healing necessary to remove her blocks to being with someone warm and attentive. She had been single on and off throughout her whole life and with each painful relationship she had faced up to her lessons and difficulties and she was able to dissolve her karma, understand the learnings and move on. At the time of meeting the new man she was 48-years-old.

Something made me ask her if she had ever read the *Celestine Prophecy* and I pointed out that within its pages, it contained the concept that we align with one of our parents and complete their uncompleted business. I suddenly felt the presence of her deceased mother, very close to my left hand side. I did not sense that the lady in front of me was meant to receive the information from her mother, but that her higher consciousness wanted her to pick it up by herself. She obviously wanted to hear from her mother and was disappointed when I told her that she had to find the hidden piece of the puzzle herself.

I let her settle and then asked her which parent she felt in tune with. She replied her mother. I then asked her what her mother had not completed. Initially she looked blank. I asked her where she had experienced the most challenges in her own life and she said relationships and making enough money. I asked if she thought her mother had ever felt that she had enough money and she said "no." By this point I felt as if we were getting somewhere. I asked if she felt her mother had ever had a fulfilling relationship and she said "no."

Her mother's spirit remained silent, listening to every word we said. The lady told me that her mother had reared six children on her own and that her father had died when she was seven. Suddenly she got it! She realised that her mother had been forty-one when she had been born and her father had died when she was seven. Added together, the two numbers made forty-eight, her current age, which enabled her to enter the relationship of her life. She knew she would marry this man. Was this destiny or free will? A numerologist could come up with the answer to this one.

The Numbers Need to Add Up

Let me give you another example. My own writing career started when I was sixty-two, the age at which my father – the parent I most aligned to – was forced to stop work. Since having children he had spent his entire life working to bring in enough money, doing a job which he disliked intensely. Music was the love of his life. My father came to me in spirit and showed me his pain at leaving the house each evening to collect insurance premiums from the back streets of London's East End. His job took him to some very unsavoury places. He always dressed very well and presented himself in a polite manner, something he found extremely difficult to maintain night after night amongst poor people and villains.

Before he married he had been a musician and longed to return to music, but his creativity was stifled. That day, I realised that I was fulfilling the missing link for him by becoming creative. I began to attract many new creative friends and acquaintances and my world was suddenly full of creativity. I was to finish the creative work that he could not complete. Is this destiny or free will?

Consider Your Client's Destiny

I am explaining these two situations in depth because I want you to realise that if you give a reading to someone, their destiny needs to be taken into account. Always look at the theme of their reading and if you ask a few questions at the outset you will get a much better idea of where you are going. Yes, of course, there is free will. The lady in question could have decided not to marry, but I doubt it. She was ready and she had completed her cycle of independence. Had she met this man six months earlier the marriage would not have gone ahead. Those studying Kabbalah (Jewish Mysticism) believe that we are here to transcend our astrological charts and I am inclined to agree. I do, however, believe that this possibility is open to just a few privileged souls at this moment of planetary consciousness; to those who are aware enough to hear this information. These souls will be in a position of fast evolution, rapidly clearing and rising above their karma.

22

The Ascended Masters

Ascended Masters are also angels and some angels are Ascended Masters. An Ascended Master is a higher being who was once living on this Earth inside a physical body, whereas angels have not lived here. To ascend they have faced many spiritual battles. With tenacity and Divine help, they have passed those spiritual trials and reached a state of God realisation. Ascended Masters reside on the higher spiritual planes in the angelic kingdoms and help you from this elevated position. Like you and I, they come in all different shapes and sizes. Their origins include many different backgrounds and religions. You may recognise some of the more well known Ascended Masters such as Jesus, Buddha and Moses. Others, like Yogananda, an Indian Yogi who brought spirituality to the west in 1920, and Saint Therese, a saint from France who died in 1997, are not so well known. There are also Ascended Masters that deal directly with psychic development, such as Saint Germain, the Wonderman of Europe, Thoth, the Egyptian God of High Magic, Merlin the Powerful Magician and Apollo, the Sun God of Prophecy.

I have included these powerful beings in your psychic development because if you ask them to come and help you grow psychically and spiritually, they will willingly do so. They want to help you reach your highest spiritual potential as then you will be a useful channel for others and the planet. You will also love yourself more and have a definite direction. They will help you to assist others and they will definitely protect you. Saint Germain is well known for his use of the ultra violet flame, given to him in 1987 to heal and protect. It is also uplifting to know that you have these wonderful deities close to you, working with you, or alongside you. Whenever you think of them, you immediately place yourself into their loving vibrations. Whatever you concentrate on, you will get more of in your life, so why not focus on the best?

Communicate With the Ascended Masters

Calling upon an Ascended Master to help you is not the same as worshipping them. It is more like having a conversation about what you would like to achieve and for what purpose. The exciting thing about this is that you can communicate with any of them and develop a personal relationship. To align with them, you need to come from an open heart and a sincere place from deep within. You do not have to pray continually or be a particularly good person to do this. Just be yourself. They will still come forward with devoted love and protection.

In the olden days, these deities were worshipped. Nowadays, we do not worship them, but we do give them appreciation – it is different. In India and around the world, there are many thousands of devotees who appreciate the love of their spiritual leaders and ascended masters. For many years, I could never understand why they were so devoted. I believed that it meant a loss of self and that the devotees were somehow shirking their spiritual responsibilities by constant devotion and handing their lives to another. I have since learned that adoration and devotion are the highest form of love we know. Hate is the lowest.

Sai Baba

Ten days after the death of Sri Sathya Sai Baba, I attended the festival of Easwaramma Day. It takes place on 6th May, on the anniversary of Easwaramma's death in 1972. It was a special and loving evening in honour of Easwaramma, the Divine Mother. Food was carefully prepared. It was also a day for feeding the poor and for children's appreciation of their parents. On arrival in the quietly lit meditation room in central London, I heard a recording of Sai Baba chanting. I did not know who I was listening to. I then saw a bright peachy orange energy descend and heard a buzzing noise on the right hand side of the room. The energy turned the most beautiful gold colour, transforming the entire room with Divine Love. It was a truly wonderful moment, made even more special for me as I had not recognised that it was the energy of Sai Baba.

Sai Baba did not appear in person to me; instead his powerful energy lit up the room. I am used to seeing angels, archangels, deities and Spirit so just experiencing the energy of an avatar was a first and far more powerful than clairvoyantly seeing. The peachy gold energy force was literally vibrating. I instantly appreciated the enormity of the Divine Love in the room and in all those special devotees who were participating. I felt enormously privileged to have been invited there by these kind and loving people and I sensed a great wave of appreciation flood my heart.

Love and Appreciation

Appreciation is a warm and loving energy that expresses gratitude for love. Appreciation always has a positive effect upon whomever you appreciate. It has been found that a ratio of appreciation of five to one is necessary to hold a friendship or a relationship close. The other person needs to hear five appreciations to feel whole and truly loved by you and you need to receive five appreciations back either from them, or more importantly yourself. Think about five things you could appreciate in your chosen ascended master guide and how those five things could have a positive outcome in your life. You can also appreciate yourself for something you have done. Appreciate yourself five times each day and your world will change. You will love yourself more and that love will go out to others and come back to you tenfold.

It is said that God is everywhere, particularly within the deities, so they are at one with God. By linking to them you bring elevated energies to you for your spiritual and psychic pathway. You will bring love, faith, kindness, elation, confidence, grace, unity, tranquillity, abundance, wonder, inspiration and courage. These wonderful beings will protect you and keep you safe, which is absolutely essential for any developing psychic. I will explain this in more detail in the chapter on psychic protection.

Psychically Extend Your Senses

When you were a child you could probably pick up information psychically through your existing five senses. You may have been highly intuitive and able to momentarily access information about the past and the future from other dimensions using your sixth sense. Children often talk of seeing spirit and angels. You may have lost this ability as you grew older and began to rationalise with your logical mind.

The major forces that transmit through your five senses are telepathy (mind to mind communication), clairaudience (hearing what is not present), clairsentience (sensing something psychically), clairvoyance (seeing people and places in other dimensions), and psychometry (accessing information by touch).

Psychometry

The simplest way to extend your psychic senses is via psychometry, the use of psychic touch. Psychometry means using an object to pick up psychic impressions from the past, present or future. The item may be something personal, such as a watch or ring, an old photograph, or a family treasure. It is amazing, but objects are able to contain psychic energy indefinitely. Stones from sacred sites or battlefields can be held and the information can be interpreted by a medium many thousands of years after an event and hundreds of miles away from their origins. An article that has remained in a family for many generations can even contain the whole history of that family; much like an old reel of film holds pictures and sounds. Violent events hold the strongest impressions due to the emotions involved. Psychometry can invoke clairsentience (psychic touch), clairvoyance (psychic seeing) and clairaudience (psychic hearing). Some mediums use this form of psychic reading because they find they work better with a personal object than without.

To practice psychometry, you will need a friend or family member who knows a great deal about the object you are going to read from. He or she must not tell you anything until you have finalised your reading. Turn the object over in your hands as you sense its energy. You may move it close to your cheek to receive more information. You may also be drawn to hold it to one side of your face rather than the other. As you do this, move the object slowly backwards and forwards. You could also place it in front of your solar plexus and let your intuitive mind pick up on it. If this is your first time experimenting with psychometry, it is important to stay silent and write down all your first impressions. Anything goes. Do not analyse what you are receiving or tell yourself it is not relevant. Analysing is a left brain activity and you need to stay in your right brain. In psychometry everything you receive will be relevant so write it all down. If you think nothing is happening write that down too and move through it. Writing will ensure you stay concentrated and undisturbed so you remain in your psychic self.

As you turn the object around in your hands and tune in, you will be astonished at how much information you get from it. You may also be surprised at how accurate that information transpires to be. When some of my students give a psychometry reading for the first time, I often see them in a state of total disbelief that the information they received psychically was 100 per cent accurate. You may not understand any symbols or words that come through. You may pick up colours and not understand what they mean. You may even feel strong emotions, but if this is the case let the emotions pass through you for they cannot harm you. Emotional responses are more likely to happen if you are clairsentient (psychically very sensitive) by nature or if you are a natural healer.

Trust Your Vibes

Trust everything that comes through for it will all have a meaning. Learning how to translate the meanings may take some time. Once you have finished your reading and relayed what you have received, invite your friend to ask you to continue clarifying what you have seen. You may need to be guided to give more information. For example, if you pick up a colour, your friend must ask you what that colour means to you. What shade is it? Is it to the right or the left? Is there anything behind it or in front of it? What might the colour mean to the owner of the article? Is it to do with a building or the décor? With this depth of questioning more psychic information will come through and you will not just think that all you saw was a colour. The same applies to a word. What does the word mean to you, for example? The easiest impressions to pick up are the emotions that have transferred to the article from people or places.

Huge Leaps of Faith

I have seen psychic students make huge leaps of faith when they realise the information they brought through is correct. If this does not apply to you and you receive very little, or if nothing is correct, you will need more practice. If this makes you feel inferior, go within, find out why and heal it. Locate the thought that makes you believe you cannot do it and ask your spirit guides to heal you.

When you have gained more confidence, move from writing and speak about what you are picking up. Make sure you do not keep stopping for confirmation from your friend as this will snap you back into logic. Be careful here for your logical mind will cause a complete shutdown of incoming psychic phenomena. It is not its place to understand. Your logical mind lives in the world of conscious thought, not in the unconscious where psychic impressions reside. You will also develop a bad habit of needing confirmation each time you do a reading. You must learn to trust your hunches.

You could also try experimenting with what I call "place psychometry." Visit an ancient site or an interesting old building and pick up a stone or touch something in that place. Take a reading from it. When you are happy with the reading, move onto another stone or object. Take someone with you and ask them to do a reading on the same stone or place then compare notes. If you cannot find anyone to go with you, bring the stone back with you instead.

Jewellery is often used for psychometry. The owner's emotions and his or her story usually come to light quite easily. A cup from an old tea set is also another useful tool if it has belonged to a family for many years, although this method is a bit old nowadays. I usually ask students to bring an article of jewellery, their phone, or a set of keys into class, neatly wrapped up. I ask them to bring their article to me behind a closed door, unwrap it and put it on a plate. This way no one sees who owns the different items. I then pass the plate around and my students choose which article they would like to read. Their readings are later confirmed by each other. This is light-hearted and very effective for developing psychics.

25

Clairsentience

This ability is similar to psychometry in that it is the use of your sense antennae to pick up things like the atmosphere in a house. You may also be able to sense a deceased person's presence around their former home or a happy atmosphere around their birthday or anniversary. Smell can play an important role in picking up the energy of those departed, for example their perfume, flowers they loved, or a particular cake they liked to bake. I have smelled the anaesthetic of hospitals and even gas when Spirit has wanted to talk about their stay in these places just before their death. This is especially noticeable if they experienced a sudden, unexpected passing on the operating table.

Your psychic sense antennae are always with you so learn to trust them. You may be drawn towards some people and not others and you might not follow up on your feelings. This usually culminates in you saying to yourself, "Why didn't I listen to my intuition? I knew it was wrong to go ahead with this person." You may constantly receive gut feelings about something or someone and you do not know why, but you know you are correct. You can always feel when someone is in a bad mood or being hostile. Their energy pours harm into the atmosphere. In the same way, you can immediately sense a scary or unwelcoming place.

Old Buildings

I recently visited Blenheim Palace and I instantly felt how hard the servants had worked there during Victorian times. One young spirit manifested in a small private antechamber and approached me. The tiny young woman told me that she started at 5am and worked until 11pm. If she spilled ashes down her apron, she would have to change it immediately and put on a new, clean starched one.

She would then be responsible for ironing these aprons wielding a heavy cast iron, almost as big as her, until one o'clock at night – only to be up at 5am the next morning. I sensed her energy as exhausted, tired and trapped inside the inevitability of a servant's role. She was only 17-years-old. I asked her spiritual guardians and angels to release her soul and she was quite happy for this to occur as she wanted to move on. She had been stuck in the half world of spirit and physical form since she had died.

Old Battle Sites

Old battle sites are excellent places to visit. I remember that the energy of one such place on the west coast of Ireland was so strong that it practically bowled me over. I was drawn to Ireland during a time when I was involved in a lot of Earth healing. I had been connected to three other people the week before the trip and at that time I had no idea there would be a trip. Interestingly, one of us had three astrological planets in Earth signs, one had three planets in fire signs, one had three planets in air signs and I have three planets in the element of water. Although it appeared to be a completely spontaneous trip, too many coincidences and synchronisations pointed to a group spiritual contract. Together, we travelled the length and breadth of the west coast of Ireland healing old battle sites.

The mix of the balance of the four elements and the equal male/female balance of two men and two women made it a very successful trip. Many strange happenings occurred on that journey, including the fact that we used only one tank of petrol throughout the whole time. It seemed that Spirit were constantly filling the car with petrol as we drove.

The Tower of London is another place I visited when I first opened psychically and at that time I was more naive that I am today. I decided to travel by barge down the River Thames in much the same way as the ill-fated dukes, earls, queens and high ranking prisoners destined for the block during Tudor times – a macabre journey but one that I felt drawn to. The Tudor nobility invariably knew they would lose their heads as very few prisoners ever saw the light of day again once in the tower.

Protect yourself if you decide to go there for it is still full of disharmonic energies. The psychic energies are dark and still discharging from those who have died there throughout the ages. The place where the block was erected is still marked out. Naively I thought I could just stand there, hang out and sense the energies of those who had died. However I could not and I was quite ill for a few days afterwards. Many memories of their deaths passed through my consciousness and my dreams for healing, which felt most uncomfortable. The one prisoner that stood out for me more than any other was Lady Jane Grey who reigned for just nine days before being executed for high treason. She was nominated by King Edward to stop his sisters, Mary and Elizabeth from ascending the throne.

It can be a little difficult to completely protect yourself against such adverse psychic energy, especially if you elected to be a healer and you are not expecting trouble. I have covered this in great detail on the chapter on psychic protection. I have had a past life in Tudor times and so it is likely that I would be more affected than most. Remember, any negative impact on you would always be matched by your own consciousness. Before I arrived in the tower, I knew how the buildings and the gardens were laid out. I also knew that other beheadings occurred in the inner chambers. I knew exactly where to go to the place where they erected scaffolds for the less important prisoners. I told my companion that there would be a building with lattice windows to the right of the block on a curve and I was right because I knew about it from my past life. I had stood in that room watching the scaffolding being erected and seeing many prisoners die. I would not suggest that you spend the afternoon standing around the block to see if you can pick anything up. I think it goes without saying that you would be better off trying somewhere a little lighter and safer to test your psychic abilities.

Psychic Smells

The power of smell is often used by Spirit to make you aware of their presence. I remember the first evening of a psychic development class. New students arrived and settled in and as always they were wondering what would happen to them. I usually like to introduce myself first and then give a brief introductory talk.

On this particular occasion there was no time for that because I immediately picked up the most powerful scent of lilies. I realised the shape of the lilies were rectangular and about six foot long. Clairvoyantly, I saw a beautiful white coffin lying under the mass of flowers in the centre of the room. It was in the middle of all the students. The scent was intoxicating and I had to open the windows in the middle of winter. I was apprehensive about telling the students about this as they were new and it did not feel appropriate. But, as Spirit would have it, there was no need to have worried.

A young lady called Rachel suddenly began talking. She had picked up the strong smell of the lilies and asked me what it was. Before I could answer, her spiritual guardians eagerly swept through leaving her in no doubt whatsoever. Rachel had lost her aunty only the week before and she had psychically returned. Evidently she had chosen that evening to say "hello." Aunty's timing was absolutely spot on. Everyone seemed calm, including Rachel, so instead of discouraging her aunty, I encouraged the rest of the students to tune into the smell of the lilies and sense the presence of this lady. Three of them even managed to psychically see the coffin despite the fact that they were complete novices.

This spontaneous experience helped the students and they were fascinated. The unusual encounter had certainly convinced them of life after death more than anything I could have taught them.

Spiritual Fragrance

Everything in your environment influences you. Try becoming more aware of what I mean. If someone or something makes you feel good, open your heart to that experience and allow yourself to soak it up. If you do not, these favourable influences will have no good effect upon you. Be with the sun, the trees, the flowers and the people who compliment you. Look deeply into a rose and notice the orderliness of its petals and its colour. Inhale deeply and soak up its beautiful fragrance. Did you know that the spirits of roses are entities from the planet Venus? Roses have come here to raise our consciousness and bring beauty to the Earth. The message of the rose is one of liberation. The rose teaches humans what true love is.

Have you ever stood near someone whom you know is not wearing perfume, yet you sensed a beautifully light fragrance emanating from them? What you can smell is the scent of their spiritual clarity. This fragrance does not exist on the physical plane and so it is very pure, subtle and light. You too can improve the fragrance of your own psychic body (your aura) through deep spiritual work. This would not, of course, be to attract another person, but to attract the higher Divine beings from the celestial planes. Heavenly entities are drawn to the fragrance of a pure soul. By working on yourself spiritually you will attract a greater number of these beautiful beings.

26

Clairaudience

Psychometry and clairsentience encourage clairaudience, which is the ability to hear non-physical words or sounds from other dimensions. The word clairaudience means "clear-hearing;" a French word. With a psychic hearing ability, you can hear the voices of ghosts in a place that has strong sounds from the past. These sounds may be triggered if someone disturbed these entities. On television, ghost busters supplied with special ghost busting equipment deliberately go to supposedly haunted places to provoke Spirit. They do this to prove the existence of Spirit in that place. They sometimes hear tapping sounds or movement frequencies, which they can measure in waves on their special equipment. Their machines look like the machines used to monitor someone's heartbeat.

Begin by noticing small but subtle signs. Have you been receiving psychic impressions without realising it? They may even come through your own voice. This can sometimes be confusing, especially if you are expecting the voice to be totally different from your own. Not every psychic can hear clairaudiently, although after clairsentience it is the most common mode of communication with Spirit. For those who can psychically hear, deceased relatives can really sound like they did when they were alive. You will know it is definitely them because they will use their own words and expressions to speak with you. If you are good enough to relay a message for someone else, Spirit will also bring through habits, likes and dislikes which your client will recognise. A good medium will usually be able to do this and you will know who it is because of the familiarity of their words. Some mediums also make certain gestures or walk like the deceased.

You can try clairaudience out for yourself by asking Spirit a question either mentally or out loud. You could direct your question to your Higher Self and wait to hear what is being said. The response may come through your own voice and yet you would know that you did not know the answer to your question beforehand. Trust Spirit enough to communicate. They know what they are doing.

I often use clairaudience to ask about someone who has come to see me. Sure enough, if I wait and remain calm for long enough, an answer always come through. When waiting for information to come through clairaudiently, expect pauses. It is slower than psychic seeing or sensing something. The trick is learning to wait through the pauses for the next round of information to come through. The answer can sometimes be very subtle and almost inaudible depending on the personality of the spirit. A warning voice, however, is stronger and more driven and may also impress an emotion of urgency upon you.

On the occasions when I have not known what to do about a problem and have completely handed it over to Spirit, the answer is usually nothing like I expect it to be. Many of those who have witnessed this occur have seen the surprised expression on my face when I received the answer. This is useful for helping people and it will make you a very accurate psychic. If you do not get an answer, you may be blocking yourself or you may not be meant to receive an answer to the question. In that case be honest with yourself and say so, especially if you are giving a reading. Never worry your client if you do not receive an answer. Sometimes there is no answer because the client needs to live some karma.

Isolate a Sound

One way of fine tuning clairaudience is to isolate a single sound from many others. As you become more confident with your psychic hearing, you will naturally be able to distinguish between anxiety or wishful thinking and a true warning coming from a clear spiritual space. Practice isolating one sound. Try this in a very busy shopping centre. Allow the other sounds to distance themselves as you raise your concentration on the sound you have chosen to focus on. Let the sound keep on coming to you.

Spend some quiet time alone as well. Silence has a sound. The more time you spend in silence the more you will understand what I mean. I first heard the sound of silence in a pine forest in Germany, where I was working in a tiny village in the countryside. It is very important to find quiet time if you wish to develop psychically. A busy mind will not notice the subtle messages. Listen to the trees. Pine trees, especially, are sacred to Cybele, the Phrygian Mother of the Gods and they will talk to you when the wind dies down. The oak tree was thought to be good for prophesising by the Druids. Stones also talk and they were sacred to the Greek Father God Zeus. In ancient times, prophecies were made from the sound of running water on the stones.

Trust Your Inner Voice

The more you trust the information you receive through your inner voice, the more information Spirit will trust you with. Spirit are watching your every move and will know if you are entirely open and honest about wanting to progress. They want to help you and will do so as much as they can. If you need to make a decision, verbalise the question and let Spirit take over and broadcast it through the ethers. You will to need to step out of the way completely and if you wait you will be amazed at the wisdom of the responses you receive. Once answered, you can then ask who is sending the impressions to you. That way you may also see the entity involved. You can, of course, be precise about who you ask to speak with you as well. Settle this before you ask for a message, for simplicity's sake. When you have tried this method of communication and when you have your answer, check if it is correct. Choose decisions that are initially non life-threatening. As you trust Spirit your confidence will grow and they will seek you out to work with them more frequently.

If you do not get a reply, dig deep within you and look for any blocks or doubts you have with trust or ability. You can do this by finding the part of you with the doubts. Set it to one side, talk to it and listen to what it has to say until all the doubts dissolve. When attempting to channel, make sure you ask for high, clear Spirit to come through and that you are protected. Your own thoughts about knowing that you only attract caring and good spirit are important here. Remember, if you are afraid you may well attract what you fear. The power of the negativity of your own expectations is what to watch for here. Not the idea of attracting an evil spirit.

27

Clairvoyance

Clairvoyance means far-seeing or clear-seeing. It is usually associated with being able to see into the future or the distant past. Remote viewing, the use of distance viewing, has been scientifically tested with incredible results. I have taught psychic students to leave their house and remotely travel through the ethers into other people's houses and come back laden with details of the contents of those houses and how the furniture is arranged. This is a relatively easy exercise. If you are developing as a clairvoyant, you may begin to see images or symbols come to mind. Initially, although you may be able to see, you may not be able to interpret what those symbols mean. When psychically seeing things, if you do not understand what you are being shown, ask Spirit to clarify. A list of some two hundred symbols for scrying (looking at an object with a reflective surface such as water or a mirror) is available on the internet or in advanced psychic development books. Please trust your own intuition, however. Remember, you are learning to interpret in your own unique way. Although books and teachers can guide you, taking a risk and striking out on your own is what will make you a good psychic. Spirit use your own past experiences to work with you through symbols and that is why it is such an individual process.

Clairvoyance and Clairsentience

You could see something and get feelings about an event at the same time. This is a combination of clairvoyance and clairsentience. You may also see someone as well as hear them talk to you. This is a combination of clairvoyance and clairaudience. I can operate through all three at once and so will you if you are willing to practice.

The first time I received psychic information through symbols was associated with someone's health (body scanning). I was shown a white business envelope with reddish skin-coloured blanket stitching around the closed flap. When I looked again, a moment later, the envelope had changed and the reddish skin-coloured stitches were being painted over with white paint so that only the faintest hint of them remained. I then saw the number six float in front of me and a hospital bed. After a long pause, I finally heard the word appendix. I asked the enquirer if they had had an operation on their appendix six weeks ago. They said "yes" and I was able to confirm that the stitches were now completely healed. I relate to the long pause again as it sometimes happens that way. You may receive half a message and need to wait for the whole message to come through. If you get stuck halfway, ask Spirit to clarify what they are trying to relay to you.

A Crystal Ball

You may feel drawn to looking into a crystal ball or mirror to see images either on the shiny surface or in your mind's eye although this method of psychic clairvoyance is a bit old-fashioned. Crystal ball readers are quite a rare breed. Nostradamus, the fourteenth century seer, used a bowl of water on a brass tripod to look forward ten centuries. He is well known for his accurate prophecies, which were encoded in rhyme. He did not, however, believe that the future was fixed in stone.

On a lighter note, I once met a crystal ball gazer with blazing long red hair wearing a beautiful emerald green velvet gown at a psychic fair. I was fascinated by her and as I watched her gazing into her crystal ball, I wondered what amazing things she could see. My fantasy was somewhat quashed later that day in the ladies' toilets where she was vigorously rubbing her neck and complaining in a strong East End accent. She told me that it gave her terrible neck ache if she did too many readings this way. I had never looked at psychic readings in this light before as I loved the fantasy of mystery too much. Although her aching neck suddenly made them less mysterious, she brought it down to Earth for me and made the whole notion of giving readings much more realistic. From then on I believed I could also do it!

Are You Visual?

Clairvoyance usually occurs more frequently in people who are naturally visual anyway. Perhaps you think more in pictures than words or you notice more details than other people around you. You might like bright colours and think very quickly. Being able to clairvoyantly see is very useful because it allows you to stay quite detached and you are unlikely to feel what you are seeing. You may later need to clear your mind of the pictures you have seen but those pictures need not impact you emotionally. You should be able to remain detached. If the psychic pictures do hang around in your mind, however, or if they are uncomfortable in any way, gather them up and send them far into the distance. Make the images small and colour them grey and black. Distort them like a television set that is not functioning properly. Finally let them disappear entirely. A tiny colourless image holds no interest to the mind of a clairvoyant. Alternatively, you could have a special place in your mind where there is a powerful ultra violet purple flame consistently burning. Throw any images onto the fire and burn them. Ascended Master, Saint Germain, keeper of the purple flame will make sure they are dissolved.

Caroline's Healing to Open Up Clairvoyance

Caroline has spent many years advancing herself through personal development. She has a wonderfully bright, infectious personality and people love to be around her. Caroline has been diligent in her approach to her spirituality and psychic development and she has spent many years attending courses. She has also spent a lot of hard-earned cash on first-class life coaches on her journey towards enlightenment. Her clairvoyant abilities had developed to an advanced state and she was far more adept as a clairvoyant than a clairaudient or clairsentient. Caroline had not been aware of this until she was placed in a class with other psychic students who were in awe of her fast mind and ability to receive symbols. Caroline's life path had been caught up with overcoming a fear of lack and needing to earn money.

When I met Caroline she could not understand why it had all taken so long and why she was still suffering with monetary problems. "This shouldn't be happening," she lamented. During a psychic money seminar, I told her that I had repeatedly heard her use these words and that I wanted to investigate this sentence.

A number of people on this particular workshop had accessed past life memories from the days of slavery when they had been involved in the maltreatment of others, taken their money and possessions and herded them onto slave ships for deportation. Caroline was the third person that day to bring up such memories.

She had lived in Africa and had been the wife of a prominent politician when the slave raids first began. The Africans had no defence because they had not anticipated that they would ever be invaded. On the first of these raids, all the fit, good-looking young men, young women and children were captured for deportation. Caroline was also taken, but her attackers did not know who she was. She might have been held for ransom otherwise.

It seemed that Caroline had been using the words, "This shouldn't be happening to me" because as the wife of a very successful African government official, she was right. Twelve years later in the cotton fields in an icy cold place somewhere in the States, she was still repeating those words. She was working nineteen hour days, she had no energy, she was thin, old and suffered from stiff joints.

I healed the trauma for her and she immediately knew that her life would improve. She had repeated the twelve years of hard work again to break the karma of being able to have money and her status back. Caroline had always yearned for the high life; expensive cars, big houses, wealth and she clearly seemed more troubled than the rest of us over this. This all made perfect sense now that we knew this about her.

Accessing this past life enabled her to use the psychic abilities she had locked up within. Releasing that past life immediately opened the universal flood gates for her to receive more income. Caroline is now extremely clairvoyant and she sees wonderful symbolic phenomena, which she is able to interpret fluently.

Heal Your Psychic Block to Clairvoyance

If any part of you feels that you should have received clairvoyance and you feel held up, this is the healing for you. Caroline, as your soul sister, has prepared the path and cleared this for you. All you have to do is step forward into your meditation, locate the doubts about your clairvoyant abilities and any emotion registering in your body and ask Archangel Raphael for help. I am sending over extra power for you to do this now. Raphael is in charge of the development of the third-eye chakra in humanity. He will bring you vision, intuition, concentration, focus and truth. He will also bring you much more certainty about your psychic gifts. Please pray deeply for these abilities so that you may help others.

28

The Aura

One of the fastest ways to prove to someone that psychic energy exists is to get them to see an aura as soon as possible. I have noticed something profound happens to doubters over and over again when they finally see an aura for the first time. This is a very easy thing to do and you can have a go on your own if you like. Place a book with a bright red cover against a white background. Sit about four or five feet away, gaze at it absent-mindedly and you will see a beautiful minty green colour emerge. Try this at twilight rather than in full sunlight and half close your eyes if you have difficulty. Focusing in this way will slow your breath right down and make you feel extremely calm. The green aura colour may well move about a bit and you could see double or even triple images. It could also seem to come and go. Just stay still and continue gazing without forcing your gaze at all. This exercise shows the existence of magnetic energy around an inanimate object and that everything has an aura, not just living things.

Another exercise you can try is to raise both your hands above your eyes about a foot away from your forehead so your fingers are almost touching then pull them away from each other. Move them towards each other and then away again. You can also try moving them from side to side. As you do this, you will see a light emitting from your fingertips. If you cannot see this, rub your hands together until they are hot. You will see the energy lines running between the ends of the fingers and how they stretch and move as you move the hands away from one another and back again. The lines are usually white. A third exercise for clairvoyance is to stretch your index and middle fingers above and slightly in front of you at a comfortable distance from your eyes. Bring the fingers towards one another until a fraction of light comes through them. Now look through the space between your fingers and you will see a dark line around both fingers. This will disappear if you move the fingers further apart.

See Your Own Aura

Seeing your own aura can be a bit tricky but it is an interesting thing to do. Look into a mirror in soft lighting then close your eyes and soften your gaze. In your imagination, picture rainbow energy circulating around your head. Take your time, making sure that you can see all seven colours of the rainbow. Now open your eyes and see what colours are still around your head; usually two will remain. If you cannot see them, ask yourself what colours they would be if you could see them and wait for an answer. Your intuition will tell you so trust it. These colours are your predominant aura for the moment. Our aura constantly changes every moment of the day.

Right now my own aura is a deep purple colour with bright golden energy around my head. This means I am intellectually involved with spiritual matters, which is correct as I am writing about psychic development. Reading auric colours will help when you want to read for others. The aura also has different levels and knowing how to see or feel these levels would enhance your ability even further.

Get Used to Seeing Colour

If you had any challenges with the previous exercises, spend some time looking at beautifully coloured materials. I sometimes visit shops full of Indian saris. In parts of London there are whole roads full of such shops, each one exhibiting hundreds of saris in wonderfully bright colours. An experience like this will lift your spirit on a dull winter's day. Why not go for a walk in a well-kept park and admire the colours of the flowers. Buy brighter clothes and bring brighter objects into your house, along with brighter foods to eat.

If you have a bright object, place it in front of you and memorise the colour then close your eyes and try to see it in your mind's eye. If you cannot, open your eyes again and take another look. Continue repeating this exercise until your psychic eye gets used to the colours and can instantly see them in your imagination.

You probably see or sense an aura every time you know someone is down or if they are in a dark mood. Conversely they may be in a sunny mood (yellow). These colours accurately describe their aura. I often ask students, "Off the top of your head, what colour is this person's aura?" Somehow everyone gets it right, so we all know how to do this instinctively even if we do not think we do. When we do not think about it too much, we know how to get a lot of answers right. If you stare at someone who feels down, you will notice they look a grey colour or an unclear darkish blue. Someone who is depressed can look like they have a murky brown colour in their auric field. Remember, you may receive this information by a knowing rather than physically seeing the colours.

Shocks and the Aura

If you sustain a shock, your aura will be impacted with that blow. If you feel very angry, dark sparks will fly off your aura. I have seen black in someone's aura when they were full of self-hatred and a thick, sludgy dark brown when someone was stuck and unable to move forward. Grey auras tend to stick with people who feel that life is boring and monotonous.

More people are aware of auras nowadays because of Kirlian photography. Kirlian was a Russian who discovered the technique of photographing auras in 1939 using a high frequency means of electronic photography. If you have ever seen one of these photos, it is highly coloured and looks like a mist is surrounding the person. The mist is usually thicker and wider in some places than others.

I have also seen photos of flowers before they were cut or when they were short of water and then again afterwards. Their auras fade. Dead leaves still show a ghost image of the missing part if they are damaged. When cut flowers are dying they need to be removed because they take energy from the atmosphere. If you grow living plants, your environment will be energised. Raw organic food often has an aura two hundred times brighter than microwaved food.

If you want to sense someone's aura, rub your hands together vigorously and then scan their body about two or three inches away from them. Keep doing this and you will automatically come across where the aura starts and stops. Your hand should bounce slightly when this happens. It may pull a little further away or go nearer the body.

If you feel down, your aura will come closer to your body. If you want your own space, your aura will tighten around you. If you feel safer and more open it will project itself out further.

Expand Your Aura

When your vitality is stronger, your aura will grow bigger. You can purposefully do this if you want to make an impact. Visualise yourself reaching to the far corners of the room and encompassing everyone in it. Your aura will immediately expand and fill the entire space. When someone has to speak in front of a large audience, their aura will become very large and it will cover the energy field of the entire audience. If that person is a good speaker, everyone in the room will be fully engaged in what they are saying. I recently attended a talk on communication. The speaker was American and very experienced. I left feeling that the message had been personally delivered to me. She touched everyone in the room with her huge, expanded aura and her open heart.

Protect Your Aura

In small, cramped places, such as the underground, you can pull your aura in simply by thinking this. Try this if you wish for some privacy. Imagine diving under your duvet, bringing the covers over your head and feeling warm and cosy. Being entirely absorbed in a book will have the same effect. When you are reading you are occupied in a small space within the pages of your book and in your imagination you have gone elsewhere. You have excluded all that is going on around you and your aura will calm and close in. You can widen your aura if you want to heal others by making your energy beautiful and expanding your thought force outwards. If you add light and send it to others, your aura will expand even further. Try this when you are on the underground. When we expand our energy with light and send that beautiful loving energy to others, we are protected at the highest level. This is the opposite from pulling in, but it is infinitely more effective.

I have included information in this book about how you can psychically own your unique space within an environment by creating Earth and cosmic energies around you. This is not the same as owning the space around you as that would compete with others. It is about creating your own psychic energy space to occupy wherever you find yourself.

Aura Colours

Being able to read the aura is crucial for psychic development and it is important to know how the colours of the aura affect us. As well as the changing colours in your aura, you will have a predominant aura colour which your soul has chosen for you to develop specific personality traits throughout your life. Each of the colours means something entirely different.

RED

I am a red person. Red people have to overcome survival issues; they have a lot of energy and they are born leaders. Their soul path is about courage. They will face many obstacles throughout their lives until they courageously move through them without anger or aggression. Red in your aura means you are a very creative person. It can vary in shade from brilliant scarlet to deep ruby. A red aura usually means you are physically active. If the red is murky there can be suppressed anger in you. Red people like to get out there and be challenged by life, especially with money and safety issues.

ORANGE

Orange people are working through issues of past trauma and shock. They need to improve their self-value and learn to embrace their creativity, optimism and independence. They are usually a people person and independent. Pale orange can signify that you are uncertain or have a low sense of self-worth.

YELLOW

Yellow people are moving away from confusion, allergies, eating disorders and rebelliousness. These people can sometimes have a sharp tongue. They are learning to spread joy and usually they are unemotional, academically bright, intellectual and have a sunny disposition. Yellow is the colour for communication. If your aura is golden yellow, you are open and creative with a keen intellect. If the yellow is a dull shade you could be secretive and dishonest.

GREEN

Green people have difficulty expressing their anger as they are overcoming envy and jealousy. They often suffer from a lack of boundaries and they can feel overwhelmed. They are learning harmony and balance, a forward direction and decision making. As they progress, they will become flexible and courteous human beings. Green is about your heart and your emotions. If you are in love, your aura will be clear green, which is a good sign of fidelity and friendship. If your aura veers towards pale green you could be a bit too dependent. A dull, muddy green aura hides conflicting emotions. Yellow-green is a sign of possessiveness and jealousy.

BLUE

Blue people are hoarders and they may find it difficult to express themselves. They must overcome high stress levels and learn to be heard. They are learning to communicate, embrace security and become dependable. Blue revolves around principles, justice and ideals. Bright blue means you put your principles before self gain. My Kirlian photo contained a great deal of navy blue, which suggests an unworldly quality. If your aura is dull blue, your need for convention might be quite rigid.

PURPLE

Purple people may have been spiritually arrogant in past lives. They are prone to depression and they may be judgemental in their need for perfection, often trying to rescue others. On a positive note they are working towards service, spirituality, patience, stability and becoming supportive and sincere. They feel driven by the need to help the planet and others. Purple is the colour you need more of to develop the spiritual and psychic side of your nature. Deep purple is the colour of spiritual awareness and it will become deeper as you evolve. If the purple is muddy or unclear, you may be spending too much time daydreaming.

PINK

A pink person can be self-absorbed and have money or love issues. Pink people find it difficult to receive and they tend to people please. If your aura is pink, you are learning to experience unconditional love, good mothering, develop your feminine side and gain compassion. Pink people are romantic, affectionate, charming and friendly. If your aura is pink, then you are a natural peacemaker. If it is bright pink, other people are highly receptive to you. If you have a pale but clear pink aura, you enjoy inner harmony. If misty, you tend to see another person's point of view too much, often to your own detriment.

WHITE

White is the combination of all of the other colours and it can be seen emanating from the crown of your head. It is radiant and glowing. Pure white light is the energy healers receive from the cosmos to direct to others. If there is a strong white coming through you, all the other colours in your aura will come alive and radiate a shimmering auric glow around your body.

Now that you know this information, try not to focus on the traits you find negative about a particular colour. Instead concentrate on the positives you are working towards inside that colour band. We all contain influences from each of the colours. If you wish to study colour, it will certainly help your clairvoyance skills and your ability to read for others.

29

Aura Levels

There are three main aura levels, the etheric (the spirit or astral), which is about two or three inches from the body, the emotional aura and mind/spirit aura.

Etheric Aura

Many people believe that we have a spirit body within us upon which the physical body is imposed. Your spirit body is believed to be linked to your physical body by a silver cord. When this cord is cut, it is said that you die. Some people see the spirit body or the etheric body aura as a silvery mist and others see it as an exact "dobbleganger" of you made up of ether. When someone is about to pass on, it changes to a whitey grey colour. If you sit quietly, float out of yourself and place your other self in front of you, you will be looking at your etheric. If you log onto YouTube and look up "the etheric body," you will see it shown as a transparent blueprint of the person.

Ghosts

Ghosts are made up of this same misty etheric substance. When you begin to see clairvoyantly you will see through things. The images are made of ether not matter. That is why ghosts float through walls in films and we cannot. If you are a newly emerging clairvoyant, you may not see psychic images as easily as you think you should. You may think the images should appear clearer or more solid like how you see things in the physical world. You could get confused about this and you may even believe your imagination is letting you down or that you "can't do it." This is not true, it just requires some fine tuning so you can adapt to how the information is presented to you.

Clairvoyance is subtle. It is like looking through a film of energy; the colours are lighter and more translucent. You will receive impressions more than solid forms. Some of the images will be very clear but others will not be at all clear. It takes some getting used to as you are seeing with your third eye, not your everyday eyes. I often see images coming to me from the left hand side of my body and I find myself staring intently as I watch the information unfold.

When you think about visual memories or pictures in your mind from your past or your present, your eyes go up to the top quadrants of your brain. You can test this out by asking someone who thinks in pictures what they did in their geography lesson when they were ten. Notice how they look upwards for the answer. The same will apply to you. Think about something that happened to you yesterday – the way you brushed your teeth for example. Now picture this in your mind and again, notice how your eyes go up. Now try to link into a spirit guide or wait for some psychic information. You will find yourself staring out into space, either to the left, the right or straight in front of you. The third eye operates in a totally different way than your physical eyes.

Etheric Colours

If the etheric colours in your aura are clear you will be fine, but if they are murky or dark you may be blocked in some way. If your etheric layer thins, your vitality will decrease. If your aura bulges or has black patches, there will be blockages in the organs surrounding that area. A bulge along your arm may reveal a broken limb from the past. If you spend too much time sitting inside on your computer your etheric field will deplete. Spending time in nature and looking at trees or sitting near the sea will lift you up again. When working as a medium, I usually sense that the etheric field of dead souls is heavier when they are still carrying emotional trauma from their Earth life.

Your Emotional Aura

Your emotional aura stretches out further from the body than the etheric, forming a neat oval shape. It does not follow the line of your body like the etheric does. The emotional aura is where your emotions live. The colours in this magnetic field will give you an idea of what you or another person is experiencing. A clear green indicates a level emotional mood, whereas a duller green might mean that you rely on people too much, or that you give in to others people's demands. I have seen patches of black and red around someone's heart when a wife was unable to forgive her husband's infidelity. Energy had leaked from the base chakra into her heart where rage and black hatred were present.

A yellow green colour here could imply resentment or jealousy. If this applies to you it might be a good idea to note your own inferiority and release it. I remember feeling constantly jealous of a friend until one day I realised that the problem lay within me; I was not fulfilling my own potential and I lacked the courage to take risks and move forward. When I investigated this, I remembered that I was very small as a child. As a result, I could not perform in all the sporting activities that I had wanted to as I could not keep up with the bigger girls in my class. Once this memory was released, along with the accompanying inferiority, I began to take more steps towards expanding my own creativity and I stopped comparing myself to my friend. Instead I admired the excellent qualities my friend had developed.

If you are in love, your aura will merge with your loved ones. The auras will entwine and turn a bright pink colour. If you do not like someone, your auras could collide and upset each other's emotional bodies. If you are highly intuitive or sensitive, you will have a fluid layer between your emotional body and your outer auric level for protection when you work psychically.

Your Mind and Spirit Aura

This is the outer layer, which also forms an oval. In stern people this layer can be quite unbending, while in others it is softer and open to the emotions. If this layer is fluid, you may be quite telepathic or clairvoyant. Its colours are blue and purple. If you are evolved spiritually, silver or gold colours may be present, as we see in the haloes of saints.

The other levels can also penetrate this aura. If too much green is found here then your emotions may be running your thoughts. If there is a lot of red you may be thinking angry thoughts or feel restless in your mind.

Magnetic Energy

Together with your aura, you have a magnetic field that sends out signals about you. This magnetic field is constantly influenced by your emotions and your reactions to the events taking place in your life. It is said that this magnetic field protrudes outwards from your heart, some feet away from your body. If you are holding negative emotions your magnetic field will beam these through your "attractor fields." Each attractor field would be made up of an emotion such as shame, guilt, apathy, grief, desire, anger and pride. Positive magnetic energy fields and attractor fields would contain courage, neutrality, willingness, acceptance, reason, love, joy, peace, etc. In fact every emotion is stored within this field.

It is important to understand that your attractor fields are controlled constantly by stronger magnetic fields of the same vibration. In other words you are being pulled in by the outer stronger fields. If you feel driven to achieve something, it is because you are being energetically pulled towards that which drives you like an iron filing to a magnet. You may not be aware that this is happening to you but you will certainly feel it. Obsessions have particularly strong energetic fields.

Your magnetic field can be healed together with the attractor fields, the emotional aura, the etheric and the mental and spirit layers of your aura, so that you attract more of what you want. In the same way your energy can be repaired so any external magnets controlling you lose their power over you. The universal law of attraction operates under the law that we attract what we think about. The trouble with this is that you won't know what your subconscious is thinking about and the only way you can find out is to watch how you respond to different situations. When you have uncovered the driving unconscious attractor fields and repaired them, you will think differently and attract more positive circumstances.

For example, if you realise that anger is emotionally more positive than apathy you might then see that you do not need anger when you begin to act from integrity and can see the other person's point of view. Then anger would disappear from your magnetic field; the anger attractor field would neutralise and you wouldn't be on an angry vibration anymore. You would then magnetically attract calm people into your life.

Whenever you need to bring yourself back to a calm state, close your eyes, focus on your heart and send yourself calmness and love. Your energy will settle quickly. This is the fast way to centre your magnetic field. Scientists measuring magnetic fields around the world have reported that 9/11 caused the most chaotic world energy upheaval ever. The planet also has its own magnetic field that responds to yours. When enough people have a loving intent the planet responds to that energy. Sometime ago I received a request to put out an invocation to the Ascended Masters asking them to reduce the floods taking place on the planet. Once I knew about magnetic fields and our own individual energies, I realised that it was possible to turn this dangerous flooding situation around if enough of us were willing to participate in prayer.

139

The Law of Attraction

On a more mundane level, I remember the first time I participated in a psychic fair. I was nervous, uptight and I did not understand the protocol. All around me, psychics were laying out tables full of memorabilia. One had statues of Red Indians, Buddhas and goodness knows what else. Others had pictures of spirit guides, angels and lucky charms. I arrived to an empty table and a set of tarot cards. My magnetic field was weak. My fear attractor fields were dominating my thoughts and sending out anxiety and doubt about my ability as a psychic reader.

For an hour I sat there and my magnetic energy and fear attractor fields were so strong that not one person came to see me. Absolutely everyone else was busy and it was truly remarkable how many people managed to avoid my table. The woman with the Red Indian statue and the Buddhas had a huge queue of patient devotees waiting for hours for a reading. Then suddenly from the other end of the hall, a little old lady rushed through the front door and made a beeline straight for me. She shook a dripping, bright red umbrella all over me while explaining in a downhearted voice that "everyone" had given her poor readings. My negative magnetic field was operating perfectly; I had attracted my worst fear. I asked the old lady to wait a moment while I went to the ladies and shaking from top to bottom, I desperately prayed for guidance, believing I would be exposed as a fraud.

When I returned to start the reading, the woman began to talk so rapidly that I could not find a gap in her words to interrupt her. She would not let me get a word in edgeways. She chatted for forty-five minutes solid before she finally slowed down to take a breath and then stopped. When I think about it now, I do not know how she kept going. She then got up, paid me and said she had received "the best reading in her entire life" and that she would recommend me to all of her friends.

In my prayers, God had sent help. Divine energy had softened and healed my fearful attractor field and made way for a healing to be carried out for her. Afterwards, I felt much calmer and I went on to give at least three good readings that evening. You might think that four tarot readings are not a lot for one evening's work at a psychic fair. But believe me that was plenty, especially when I had been so dreadfully frightened, completely wearing myself out with nervous tension. On the plus side, I felt it was a very successful evening and an excellent start for someone like me who at that time was a complete novice.

That day taught me to put my faith in God, my spiritual guides and angelic guardians and trust my intuition. I sensed that the old lady had needed to continue talking. Another psychic might have tried to interrupt her and got nowhere. Either way, she would not have listened because she was so totally convinced that no one could read for her. Luckily for me, it all turned out perfectly and I was on the way to becoming a better psychic.

30

Psychically Cleansing to Manifest

Manifestation is the use of your mind to make something happen for you. You may not realise that you are working *magic* when you do this but you are. Your thoughts live in the world of the ethers and your words live in the physical world. Everything you could possibly aspire to be or want to have happen already exists and someone out there either has it or is already doing it. This means you can align yourself with that outcome providing you clear any negative beliefs or psychic blocks inside of you. If you want something and it is not forthcoming, or if you are only getting a lukewarm response from your endeavours, your aura is not pure or powerful enough. Your aura contains everything that has ever happened, is happening and will happen to you, in all your past lives, your in-between lives, your parallel lives, possible lives, future lives and any other lives you can possibly think up. When you are an experienced psychic you will be able to read this wide spectrum of information in another person's aura quite easily. You will also be able to visit the higher dimensions in the ethers where the Akashic Records are kept and gain access to someone's history if that is deemed acceptable by their soul.

Purify Your Thoughts

Most of us understand that to manifest we need to think about what we would like to have happen. But did you know that thoughts live in the air and if you want your thoughts to fly through the air a long way and hit your goal spot on, they need to be strong. They need to leave you with the "oomph" and energy of a jet fighter plane roaring down the runway, geared up for take-off. Those thoughts need to be turbo-charged and ready for action! To accomplish this your aura needs to be full of light; strong and, above all, pure. A strong, pure, luminous aura will also protect you from outside interferences. A pure aura means you are actively clearing out past rubbish and junk, all those unexpressed emotions and negative thoughts.

As you progress psychically, you will realise the importance of what I have just told you. Grounding exercises are essential to keep you here in the now, in your physical body whilst you relay psychic messages, otherwise you will feel very spaced out and dizzy. I have seen psychics get sick because they fail to ground themselves. They find themselves floating around the astral plane, half in and half out, thoroughly disorientated and unable to think straight. Even so much as a tiny puff of wind of psychic interference would blow them over.

Cleansing exercises are essential to keep you free from your own psychic and emotional interference, or that of other people. If you did not clean your dustbin, the rubbish would build up and putrefy the atmosphere in a short space of time. Your home would soon smell foul and rats, vermin and flies would feast on the growing germs and bacteria. Until someone threw the rubbish away, this situation would remain. It is exactly the same when it comes to your aura. Your aura is a living consciousness, moving in and out of different energies all day long. Some of these energies are pure, loving and kind yet others are soiled, vicious and downright nasty.

In a highly dense, polluted city you will be swamped by these different psychic energies and find yourself easily contaminated by people, computers, pylons and mobile phones. When you sit on a public transport seat on a bus or train you are sitting in the aura of all those who have ever sat there, literally breathing in the emotions and thoughts of all those who have frequented the carriage.

Therefore, it is vital to do a daily clean up, but it is better still to do a purification three times a day. This will keep you physically strong, mentally alert and psychically grounded. Once your aura is wonderfully clean, bright and shining that does not mean you will never come up against another psychic interference, or that you will instantly manifest absolutely everything you conjure up. It does mean you will be able to clear any adverse energies affecting your mental, emotional and physical health and go on to manifest at greater speeds and with increased efficiency. You will have more vitality and feel more alive, sometimes without knowing why. Others will comment about your vitality because everyone can see or sense auras, they just do not realise it.

I once heard about a man who worked in an American Penitentiary where the bulk of the inmates were on death row. Since working at the prison the man had been having nightmares on a frequent basis. Each day he had to walk down long and winding corridors to reach his small office on the third floor at the other end of the sprawling prison. On his way, he passed cell after cell of men full of rage, evil, revenge, pain, remorse and suffering. He realised he had to urgently do something to protect himself. This man read up on a number of powerful cleansing and grounding exercises so that he energetically remained untouched by what was going on around him. He began to clean and energise his aura outside the prison gates on arrival and then again on departure. He cleaned his aura once more before entering his home. Each evening he hung his clothes outside or washed those that were washable and took a cold shower to get rid of any residue from his aura. His nightmares ceased.

Had this man also understood the power of transmitting light and love to the inmates, he could have made a very powerful impact on the whole prison, as well as effectively protecting himself.

Daily Aura Cleanses

Some time ago I worked in a food depot where there was a lot of unrest amongst the employees. One of them, George, had a well known reputation for stealing. At the time, I was studying to be a yoga teacher and writing many essays in slack periods of work. I was studying the Upanishads and other uplifting spiritual works. I had no idea what was going on around me in the other parts of the building. I fasted and performed daily aura cleanses and psychically cleaned the air in my room. When people came to my office, they were completely baffled by the peace that pervaded the atmosphere in that small space, since the rest of the depot was in energetic chaos. George never stole from me despite the fact that I left my bag on the floor for him to see. He treated me with the utmost respect. His stealing energy could not match mine even though he frequently stole from others. To others he was a thug and they were frightened of him. To me he was generous and kind. You will see this same phenomena take place when one person has a lot of trouble with someone while another person thinks they are wonderful. It is a mirror reflection. The people who had been stolen from in the depot either had a fear inside them of being stolen from, or they themselves had stolen from others in past lives and were paying back a karmic debt.

A Quick Cosmic Earth Cleanse

A quick cleansing routine can easily be included in your daily life. This uses the powerful mix of the Earth energies and the cosmic energies. All life is sustained by these two energies from above and below. Imagine a bright ball of green energy in your base. Drop it down into the centre of the Earth and make it into a tube, which is as wide as you wish. Once it is in place, breathe deeply and pull up pure energy from the core of the Earth through your feet. Let that pure energy flow all around your body and into your head and brain, washing out any negative

145

bits and pieces. The negativity can be thoughts, feelings, or dark impressions in your energy field. Flush the negative energy down the grounding tube back into the Earth for transformation. Watch as it cleanses and purifies. The Earth will do this naturally and it will change colour. Once it has been thoroughly cleansed, pull up more clean Earth energy through your feet and repeat this flow, circulating it around your body until your energy is clean and bright. You might find this exercise easier if you take a step forward into another place each time you draw up fresh Earth energy.

Next, raise your arms up to the sun and gather a great golden ball of energy. Using your hands, pass it down through your body, back and front and then your aura before sending it through to the Earth and down the grounding tube. Keep on drawing down large golden suns and feel the light and warmth until your aura and body are bright and clean and it feels like a balance between the Earth and the cosmic energies has been achieved. You should now be inside a nice, bright, minty, golden colour with a strong golden glow all around you that has power to bounce anything away. Dissolve the grounding tube by stepping forward and letting the Earth transform it. Tell yourself, "I am divinely protected."

Cosmic Frequencies

The whole cosmos is vibrating on different frequencies. Each time you purify your thoughts, your emotions, your physical body and your aura, you immediately align yourself with all those on a similar frequency band and you will become more psychic. Calling upon Spirit to manifest what you want to achieve is not enough. Like attracts like and you must be karmically ready to receive your psychic gifts by cultivating great purity, strength of mind and self-control.

Accessing the Earth energy and cosmic energy will connect you to the two worlds so that the current can flow freely between them. This central powerhouse in the world produces enough current, but for your own light to burn brightly, you will need to be connected to the mains. Cleansing your aura, performing grounding exercises and clearing any psychic blocks will enable you to do this. Prayer will reinforce that power, especially if you require your gifts to accelerate and be of service to others.

If you are endeavouring to be pure and luminous and your vibrations are moving towards being in harmony with heaven, all the forces of nature will understand and listen to you and they will be able to grant your requests. Otherwise you could be asking for years without getting anywhere and you may wonder why. I have seen a lot of people going through this dilemma.

Your Own Psychic Frequency

We each have our own unique psychic frequency. To operate within your frequency wherever you are and to protect yourself fully, you will need to learn how to own it.

Owning your psychic frequency does not mean you own the space; it means you can be inside a space, owning your own unique frequency.

People who own a lot of space are usually overwhelming. I am sure you have met people who seem to take up the entire room with their presence. This is not always comfortable for other people around. I have noticed that people with weight problems often do this and I have discovered that their unresolved inferiority was counter-balanced by the need to occupy too much space. Others who do not occupy enough space, such as those who are constantly apologising for their existence, can be equally trying as you will find yourself continually drawing them out and trying to make space for them. This occupation of space is energetic and not necessarily physical.

Again, you can use the forces of Mother Earth and the powerful cosmic energies to own your own psychic frequency. From the centre of your third eye, send out two lines of golden energy to the front two corners of the ceiling of your room. Then send out two lines of golden energy to the two back corners of your ceiling. Then send out two lines of green Earth energy to the floor and two lines of green energy to the back of the floor behind you. Colour in the rest of the room with the golden, green light frequency. Fill up the space with the gold and green and mix the two energies. You are now inside your personal psychic frequency.

31

Cleanse Your Words

Sometimes we can get so frustrated and upset that we have to let off steam. The words get trapped in our heads and conversations whirl around and around with those we have issues with. We feel resentment towards these people or we feel used or blamed and as a result our emotions become disturbed and out of control. When this happens to you, it will send your chakras reeling. Psychic students often ask me how they can rid themselves of these interferences without harming another. As a first step, you could write out your feelings. Sometimes this is not enough though and the words have to be said out loud if you are very upset or angry, especially if you are auditory by nature. If this happens to you, before expressing that emotional charge into the world, ask that your words are immediately dissolved into the light by spirit guides or angels. Ask that your words have no negative impact on the person with whom you are angry.

If you deliberately aim your words at that person you are actually cursing them or psychically attacking them. This is fine if that is where you are and if you are unable to forgive. It will, however, hold your psychic development up because your mind will be involved with adverse energies. Spirit and your Higher Wisdom require that you are calm in order to use you as a channel. Please also remember that by universal law your words and deeds must boomerang back.

A spiteful, angry word is like a missile that travels through space, triggering forces, disturbing entities and causing irreversible effects. If it is an evil, nasty word, the damage it does is irreparable. Take care, for you will be rewarded for your good words but you will have to karmically pay for your bad words. You can never retrieve the words you have uttered.

The Law of Karma

Many budding psychics do not understand how the Law of Karma works. They do not realise that their spiritual growth will accelerate many times over as they psychically open. They allow their feelings to boil over and say whatever goes on in their minds about another. But one day Karma comes knocking on the door and it is payback time. These people think it is sufficient to apologise for their behaviour, however, this is not so, because by Karmic Law all ill effects must be rectified. If you steal from someone, you will need to pay back that person either in this lifetime or another. Only then will you be free of the karma. Forgiveness releases the person who has been wronged and if this is you, you will find a sense of relief by forgiving yourself and the other, but it does not release the culprit. If you are the culprit, you will need to atone for your actions.

When giving psychic readings try to get Spirit to give you sound advice, which is fair to all parties. It is easy to side with someone when they appear to have been badly treated, but it must be remembered that these people are living out their karma so what has been happening is appropriate or they would not be experiencing it. As far as possible, try to remain neutral to the outcome of their reading.

I once gave a reading to a woman who was sleeping with four men. Initially, I had difficulty in reading for her as I had a moral judgment, but then I got out of the way and a higher truth came through. Because of my closed attitude, I had not realised that all five of these souls were being healed from this experience. This lady's self-esteem was being healed as she encountered the closeness with the four men. At that point I realised that it was crucial to stay out of the way even if it did not fit my own values. That way I could offer the best unbiased psychic advice. Staying neutral is not always easy, but if you operate from the premise that you wish to work for the light and for the good of all of those concerned, you cannot go far wrong.

Refuse to participate in any gossip whatsoever and you will clear up your karma at lightning speed. Focus your thoughts on helping people and bring God's light to them and your psychic abilities will soar. Make it a habit to thank Spirit and the Angels after every reading so you build a familiarity with their energies and a good rapport with your own spiritual guides. Talk to them constantly so they know who you are. Cleanse your aura daily so you light up. That way, they will find you easily.

The Power of Blessings

If you bless those you know and the things you touch, it will become a Divine habit. Say words that inspire and uplift your friends and colleagues and you will see the effects of the good words you sow. Try saying, "I appreciate you" more often as this works wonders. If you feel alone or neglected, repeat the word "love" over and over again, each time in a different way to trigger the cosmic forces of love to come to you. This may not be easy at first but work through the resistance and keep going. Remember, you are clearing psychic blocks in order to become the best psychic you can be. Your ego loves resistance. It likes to get in the way because it fears its own demise.

If you feel that you are groping in the dark, say the word "wisdom" over and over. If you feel directionless say the word "certain" over and over and if you feel anxious, hemmed in, or worried about money, say the word "freedom" again and again. Keep this up until you feel these words vibrating and singing in every cell in your body. Paste stickers all around your home or office and every time you see one, stand straight and smile until it becomes a habit. Down moods hold your energy down. Quickly find out why you feel down and heal it as this will allow psychic forces to operate through you.

32

Psychic Attack

Psychic attacks are a reality. There are spirits and entities that wish to harm others, just as there are humans who hurt and harm one another. The spirit world is very densely populated and it contains spirits of all backgrounds and levels. Some of the lower levels are full of disturbed souls who have got "stuck." It is also quite possible to pick up adverse energies from people who are still alive, especially if you are sensitive. Some places certainly contain more negativity than others and so do some people.

Over the years, I have worked extensively with the healing of people who have been psychically attacked. Some of them have been aware they were under threat, others have just felt odd and still more have been quite sick without knowing why. I have also been psychically attacked on a number of occasions. The first time over eighty-seven entities had to be removed from my aura. These entities were full of apprehension and fear and their energy had made me feel overly fearful. I attracted them to me because of a past life in Germany and the residue of the fear of those around me when I died was still with me floating on the astral plane and over-spilling into my aura. Entities are now leaving the planet as the light energies have increased making it impossible for them to stay.

On another occasion, a number of spirits used my energy to sustain their survival. Again, this was from the same past German incarnation where the energies were still lingering from those who had been interned and starved in the war. These entities were experiencing shock and they had no way of finding their way to the light. I was also attacked when I wanted to spread more light and love into the world. I was held up by those in spirit who did not wholly agree with this. Fortunately all of this has now been healed, although it took some determination.

Voodoo Black Magic

I came across Voodoo black magic when I worked in Africa and although the people operating it did not seem to have much power – they appeared to be naive villagers who had grown up with this type of thing – their intentions were malignant. I do not suppose they understood the karma they were incurring, under spiritual law, which states that "what leaves you in the way of harsh words, gossip, evil thoughts and nasty actions will return to you." In Africa, as well as elsewhere, miniature dolls are still being used to psychically attack. I know because I saw a small replica made to look like my friend, Megan, who was being attacked. Interestingly, the doll had a blaze of red hair, just like her.

I realised that this negative experience had been brought to my attention for the purpose of healing not only the African ladies who were initiating the psychic attack, but also Megan, who was at the receiving end. When I asked my spirit guides what was going on, they showed me a number of past lives where Megan had been cruel and vindictive to many people in Africa, which was now up for correction. The timing was perfect. She had recently got involved with a young African and had decided to marry him. She knew deep in her heart that she "owed" this young man something. Nothing anyone said to her could deter her from going ahead with this marriage, even though it was obvious that it would not last. He and his entire family were going to benefit enormously from a continual financial input. I believe it was fate.

Megan told me she did not expect to be married for more than five years, during which time he would become a British Citizen and gain the freedom to come and go as he pleased. In a previous lifetime I saw that she had taken his and the other family members' freedom. She had brutally punished them and made them work long hard hours. She had also been involved in slave trading and she had made a fortune at the expense of these poor people. At some level, they all recognised each other again. A psychic healing was carried out and it all subsided. The attacks stopped and they all became friends. The young African man left her just over six years later and went on to marry an African girl once he had received his papers. Although heartbroken, Megan realised that it was payback time.

Free Floating Entities and Ghosts

Psychic attack can also come in the way of free floating entities that fasten themselves to an individual. If someone's aura is weak, or if they have been drinking or taking drugs, they will be more prone to this type of attack. This is especially prevalent in people who black out completely from binge drinking or drug taking, leaving themselves unconscious and open to these adverse energies.

If you psychically attack another with your words or gossip, that energy circulates around you and builds up. If that person does not retaliate and sends you back love, the build up can grow more intense. You will then attract a psychic gossip cloud and put yourself on the same vibration as all those operating from that state. This is pretty dangerous stuff.

I have spoken about words and their power in an earlier chapter and I would urge you to be cautious about what you think and say from now on. If you have an issue, it is usually coming from somewhere in the past. Usually the person with whom you are angry or hurt is not the original perpetrator of the crime, unless there is a past life connection like the one I have just spoken about. I mentioned in another chapter that the way to get rid of these words and anger is to express them, but carefully ask that these words be "neutralised with love" by the Divine before letting them go into the air.

Ghosts can also hang around close to Earth. Some of them linger on the lower astral planes. They can be troubled and need to move on, but they get stuck because they are unsettled and feel they have unfinished business here. As we are now seeing from television programmes on haunted places and houses, some of these entities can be very disturbed. The best way to deal with them is to speak to them and listen to their complaint. This will take some courage, but if you can do this you will find that they usually calm down and heal. If you are afraid, pray and ask for help. Ghosts are often extremely protective of a house or a place where they have lived. They may also come forward if they were married and their wife or husband is marrying another person. I have also known ghosts who have felt very unsettled because they have seen their wills tampered with or their loved ones squander their hard-earned cash. Make sure you have psychic healing if you feel afraid so that you remain calm if one of these entities approaches you. That way you will stay centred and able to cope.

If you constantly read unhappy stories in the papers or watch unhappiness on the news, you will draw "unhappy" energies to yourself from the Earth world and the spiritual dimension. That is the law of attraction. We attract what we focus on. Try to still your mind with as much positivity as you can.

Cleansing Evil

In occult and mystic teachings, evil plays a part as a force and it is directly opposed with the energies of love and light. Most of us are afraid of evil in some way and all of us have had nightmares. You may have awoken from a dream feeling completely terrified and knowing that the fear was too great to have been your own. Throughout the world, there are places thick with evil and full of sick and frightening vibrations. War zones, for example, carry terror, fear and torture.

I have always been open in my workshops with students over the subject of evil and I have never tried to hide its existence, for otherwise they would not be protected. There are lots of techniques available to shield and protect yourself from evil, but if you understand it more readily, it will bring you to a more mature state of being.

Evil appears to consist of two things: the natural cosmic force and human behaviour. Cosmically we live through growth, maturity, decay and destruction, which is the cycle of life. It is normal that there is death, loss of your physical body and then decay of that body. The life force within you will one day break down and disperse. This applies to anything living, as well as the stars and galaxies. When an animal or human dies and decays, the flesh rots, putrefies and smells. For us the smell of rotting flesh is most unpleasant. Compost heaps full of plants smell much more pleasant. Did you know that in the Hindu religion, there is a specific Goddess who deals with the cosmic rhythm of decay and destruction? Her name is Kali and she is the female deity of destruction and organic disintegration who finally devours everything, thus transforming it.

The second force in evil is the effect that evil has on a certain type of human behaviour. This behaviour is a twisted annihilation of life executed with pleasure. It happens when overdoses of resentment, anger and hatred combine with the natural energies of decay and destruction.

It is normal for us all to have moods of depression, anger and sometimes destruction and aggression. Imagine though, if you were suddenly hooked up to a powerful cosmic force of destruction, which is everywhere and very powerful. You could get mixed up in it. That level of mix, combined with your own destructive mood and the powerful universal force of decay, could enable you to lose sense of what is right and what is wrong. The worst scenario here is that some people actually get involved with this destructive force and go on to enjoy the destruction. We all know of people who inflict pain on others as we read about it everyday in the newspapers. This results in abuse, rape, torture and death. Such behaviour is what we would label "evil."

Evil situations are also filled with the pain of the victims and these energies float up to make great psychic clouds of evil vibrations. Every time someone is raped or tortured anywhere in the world this psychic energy field is being fed.

Evil is very different from normal negative emotions. It is very real and it is all around us. The best way to defend yourself against evil is to concentrate on your loving spiritual practices. Constantly train your mind and energy towards good if you can.

The Christ and the Cosmic Love

If you ever come across evil, you will realise just how potent being connected to the Divine Ascended Masters can be. Always draw upon the pure energies of the Christ or whomever you believe to be good. Do not engage with it nor communicate with it. Put all of your attention onto the Christ and the Cosmic Love energies and bring them down into your aura. You can connect and pray over and over again for protection. Also, blast love into the situation as this will always overcome evil. If you are in a difficult situation, make the connection in a very intense way. Eliminate everything from your mind apart from your connection. Be single-minded and pray over and over. The Lord is my Shepherd is an effective prayer as its words are, "Even though I walk through the valley of the shadow of death, I will fear no evil for thou art with me." Keep going until you transform the situation into one of love. This takes some doing, but love always overcomes evil.

Fear

When you talk about fear it always feels better than keeping it bottled-up inside you. Fear is a vibrational energy rather than a mind experience, although some people would have you believe that you can use mind over matter. The effect of fear is naturally psychological, but the primary cause of fear is two vibrational fields of energy converging inside you and causing disharmony. Fear occurs when your aura meets another field of energy and the vibration of that energy field causes friction. Instead of harmony you experience a sudden sharp stab of intensity which shoots down into your nervous system and feels very uncomfortable. Fear shows you that something is occurring in your aura.

As a psychic you will work with vibrations, so fear needs to be acknowledged and accepted. After the initial impact of fear, instead of being overcome by it, see if you can allow it to pass through. To do this you must mentally step back and observe what is happening. Centre yourself and move your hand round and round your stomach in the opposite direction of the fear. Keep your body moving, as this will help to move the fear vibration through. Observe that your body, your aura and your consciousness are dealing with a fear energy vibration and that this will not kill you. If you are panicking, let the first intense waves of panic pass through you, breathing deeply and slowly. You could say out loud, "I am frightened because ..." and keep on coming up with answers until the fear subsides. Then use your name and say "(your name) is frightened because..." Keep answering until you run out of things to say. If you are alone, talk to Spirit, or to the wall. If you are with a friend ask them to hold the energy for you whilst you do this. Some powerful causes come from the subconscious this way and you will learn a lot about yourself.

Overcoming Fear

In some spiritual schools the students are placed in frightening places such as cemeteries and they are surrounded by corpses. The students learn to stay centred whilst strange, terrifying vibrations occur in their auras. Sooner or later they learn to be unruffled and impartial about their feelings. This can be a difficult experience but it usually leads to a welcome level of freedom. I do not advocate this type of experience for anyone reading this book, but it is useful to know about these things.

There is a technique used by the Buddhists that works with fear. Come into your perfect centre, purposefully drawing the energy of the uncomfortable vibration until you can feel it inside you. Hold your perfect centre, as now you are going to absorb the energy and at the same time, transform it. Concentrate fully and when you feel the fear, pain, or anxiety, instead of letting it rush through you, breathe your calm consciousness over it. As you absorb the negativity, send it love and harmony and start to bless it. Using this method it is possible to calm down a screaming child. It is vital that you stay centred and calm.

Another technique you can use is to let the Earth absorb the fear. Imagine a spinning plug-hole in the middle of the fear, through which the negative energy is sucked into the Earth. As you watch this take place, you feel it draining away. Always ask the Earth if this is okay beforehand and afterwards thank her for transforming the fear.

Do not use any of these techniques for huge, evil energies or those that are too much for you. Be kind to yourself and remember to call upon the Ascended Masters to take over in times of trouble.

Overcoming Fear of Loss

Many years ago I stayed with some spiritual people in Wales who noticed I had a fear of losing my money. They had me sit in a tea shop about ten feet away from my parked car, in which

I had purposefully left my handbag. Many people passed the car and stared at the bag. Each time this happened, a huge wave of fear swept over me and this occurred many times during the next hour until the fear gradually subsided. One man even picked the bag up and then put it back.

Finally I calmed down and trusted that the bag and its contents were safe and would remain so. This exercise helped me to trust that nothing could ever be stolen from me again unless I karmically owed the money to someone. At the time, I lived in a cottage overlooking allotments, which consisted of open farmland behind the house. During the time I lived there, I never once locked either my car or my house as I knew I was totally safe. Insurance companies are making huge sums of money because people are frightened. As you progress psychically and energetically, you will come to understand that you are totally protected by your spirit guardians and guides and that nothing can harm you except for your own fearful thoughts.

33

Psychic Protection

There are many methods of protecting yourself psychically, one of which is to ensure that your aura is cleansed daily. Fresh air, healthy food and daily exercise are each important to ensure you build a strong physical and etheric aura. Get out of breath everyday to bring in a fresh supply of oxygen. You would not be able to run your car without any petrol in it. Likewise, you need oxygen in order to function optimally.

A cold shower will blast away any negative energy you may have gathered, as the coldness shocks the aura. It is a fast and effective energy cleansing method. I can hear you thinking "Oh no!" but try it, because if you are tired, it will give you several hours of extra energy. If your aura is blocked and overloaded with negativity, you will slow down. Your head may feel fuzzy and your thoughts will be far too busy. Forests, the sea and open spaces in nature will clear the aura of electronic build-up. Computers and televisions strain the eyes and, if overdone, can disturb your liver and cause fluctuations in your aura, draining the etheric energy.

The Incredible Power of Mantra

As you develop, your capacity to attract spiritual energies will heighten. If your immune system is strong and your aura is clean, any difficult spirits will be more likely to bounce off your magnetic field and they will not be able to enter. Chanting mantras full of wisdom and love will cleanse your thoughts and your vital energy field. You can also chant in English if you like so you receive the full force of the words. Also, choose significant words like love and trust. Try walking along the street chanting "I am love" in your head as this will infuse the energies of love deep into your system. Keep doing this everyday. You find the time to brush your teeth everyday, so if you do the same with these protective practices, you will improve your health and live longer.

Mix With Positive People

Mix with people who are performing high spiritual practices as they will enhance you with their positive approach to life and steer you in the right direction. Constant repetition of a mantra will cause it to eventually automatically repeat itself without any conscious effort. Chanting will cleanse your chakras and flood your mind and body with powerful wisdom. Attend spiritual meetings that encourage singing and prayer to deities and absorb their energy. Absorb the vital light energies of the prayer and the wonderful uplifting words. Read books on higher spiritual beings then place them under your pillow when you sleep.

Practice Yoga

Practice yoga if you can, as yoga moves the energy on all levels, balancing your endocrine system and your chakras. It will energise your physical body and store vibrant energy in your chakras. The yogic mind practices breathing techniques, which will reduce mental distractions and leave you calm and settled.

In the ancient yoga texts it is written that there are seventy-two thousand flows or currents in your psychic body, visible as currents of light to someone who has developed their psychic vision. These currents connect the different chakras and psychic centres in your subtle body. The most important current in your psychic body is found in the centre of your spinal column. Two other important psychic channels run alongside your spine. Keeping these psychic passages clear will stabilise and centre you. There are meditations to help you achieve this. Learning the art of yogic breathing will greatly strengthen your mind, your nervous system and your body against psychic attack.

Give Yourself a Good Shake

Give your body a good shake to release blocked or stuck energy. You may come across someone who makes you feel threatened in some way or with whom you feel uncomfortable. If you do not show your feelings and instead let it all build up inside, it is likely that you will feel weary, angry or hurt after. You may also feel disappointed with yourself because you did not protect yourself beforehand. Usually you will be experiencing anxious energy that has got stuck. You must understand that to keep healthy on a psychic level you must move your body regularly. When I said shake your body I literally mean to shake your body from top to toe.

Noises are also effective for releasing psychic "gunk." A good scream, sigh or gasp will do. If you are working with a lot of people, take some time out during the day in between sessions as this way you can re-centre yourself with a quick cleansing. Use the quick cleanse mentioned above several times a day. Take ten deep breaths, forcing your breath out. At the end of the day, take off your working clothes and hang them up to air. Wash them or give them a good shake and give yourself a good stretch and shake at the same time. Have a shower or a bath and allow your body to be in the open air for a few minutes. Do not forget to release any energy which is trapped in your hair by washing it.

34

Talismans

A Talisman is an object (usually a gem, flower, ring, bracelet or pendant) which possesses a force that has been impregnated by either nature or a being of exceptional psychic power. Only those who can merge with the Supreme Being can prepare a truly effective talisman. There are also negative talismans prepared by black magicians. These objects have been impregnated with evil forces, which can be sent to people to make them ill or cause an accident or a conflict.

To prepare a talisman you must have pure intentions but remain detached from the outcome. This way you pass the intentions to the universe at the same time as coming from a neutral space – something I keep emphasising. People wear talismans for many different reasons; some to gain power, others for protection. People think the talisman will give them whatever they ask for with no effort on their part, but this is not so.

To stay powerful, a talisman must be constantly charged. You will be able to rely on a talisman only if your psychic work is in harmony with what it represents, together with the powers and virtues bestowed upon it. If you choose a talisman to help and sustain you in your spiritual endeavours, it will give you inspiration and nourishment. However, no external means can have a lasting effect on you if you do not aspire to live a sensible life. This is evident when you see people wearing crosses around their necks, yet their lives continue to be sad and miserable. Wearing the cross has done nothing to help them. To make that cross come alive it will need to be imbued with love and faith.

Sacred Places and Talismans

Sacred places have also become talismans because of the energies of the stones or the saints or deities that have lived or worked there. These enlightened beings have left their beautiful light imprints on these sacred buildings, rivers or stones. People can be healed and others can receive revelations that transform their lives from these places, but they need to be carefully protected. However holy and pure these places are, they can be sullied if left open to the negative forces of darkness.

Deities and Talismans

One of the most powerful exercises I use with my students is when I ask them to bring the picture of a deity to class – preferably one who is still alive – then to gaze into the eyes of that enlightened soul. I have found this works better if the deity is young and in their prime. If you do this and breathe quietly whilst doing so, you will receive a wonderful upsurge in your energy. Allow the energy from their eyes to pour through you and throughout your aura. Do this a number of times a day and you will naturally align to their beautiful energy even when you are elsewhere.

Become Your Own Talisman

I am not going to say much more about talismans as I believe that by working on yourself through healing, prayer and cleansing, you will become your own talisman. You co-create with the Ascended Masters by matching your own light vibrations to theirs, via constant prayer. This is how they can help you. They will encourage you to empower yourself and to eat correctly so your body transforms into an excellent source of power, filling it with love and wisdom to fulfill your mission. Spiritual ascension is about finding your true purpose, developing your psychic gifts and other qualities you need to fulfill it and constantly co-creating with the masters to attain it here on Earth. It is not about floating off to heaven.

35

Signs you are Opening Psychically

Dreams Become More Vivid

As you continue to develop, you may find that you dream more vividly than before. You will see more colours and you may even feel emotional when you wake up. You might awaken in the night and feel wide awake for no apparent reason. A favourite time for this seems to be 4am; it is said this is the hour for "witches" to wake. You may have been a witch in a past life. I know I have.

Many healers and psychics were persecuted throughout Holland, France, Spain and the British Isles for hundreds of years as their abilities were seen as suspicious. Thousands of innocent young women were burned for no apparent reason other than because they helped others. These young women have since reincarnated and are scattered throughout the world. They obviously still possess their gifts especially if they have agreed to use them again. They may feel very frightened of doing so, however, because of past persecution. This can all be healed and it is usually fairly easy for these people to develop.

Premonitions

You may have started dreaming of events before they take place or receiving messages in your dreams about people close to you. It could be that you cannot pass these messages on for fear that the recipients will think you have no business doing so. You may also feel worried that they will think you are odd in some way, especially if you work with them or if they are family members. If this happens, you could be keeping the messages to yourself instead of passing them on. If this resonates with you and you do not feel it is appropriate to pass on a message, either tell someone else without giving names or write the message down so that you do not keep it stored inside you. You can dispose of the paper by shredding it, burning it, or typing it out on your computer then deleting it. This keeps the psychic flow moving. Spirit will know if you are worried and the source of psychic messages could dry up if you do not enable them to flow through you and out the other side. It is never a good idea to keep things inside you, which is especially true if a spirit is urgently trying to get you to warn someone.

A good psychic is able to bring a message through and forget its contents within a few seconds. If someone asks me to repeat a message even a few seconds later, I cannot remember it. I have trained myself to let go of the information as soon as it comes through. In that way I am like a sieve, totally protected as I do not hold onto anything. If you are worried after reading this, go within and ask for healing.

Lucid Dreaming

Lucid dreams are those we remember easily and usually involve a half-sleeping/half-awake state, as if you know you are dreaming. The dreams will remain vivid upon waking. During this state, dead relatives can come forward and communicate and everything will seem more vivid than a normal dream.

Past Life Witchcraft

Your memories may also disturb you. You may have had past lives involving witchcraft and as a result you may feel emotional about the thought of witch burnings. From the thirteen hundreds until the seventeen hundreds healers and psychics were hounded throughout Europe and some of them were burned while others were hanged. You could have been viciously tortured for your beliefs and still be carrying the fear. The Inquisition, the Knights Templar, or the Cathar trials may still hold deep-seated fear within you. Witch hunts were commonplace back then and perhaps you are holding back from using your powers today because of that fear. Some people have problems with their throats because of the hangings and others fear fire. Despite this, you may have elected to come back, re-learn your gifts and begin to use them again, perhaps even choosing to teach. If this is the case, it is necessary that you release the fear to begin your psychic work and fulfil your destiny.

Healing For Persecution

If you sense that you have been persecuted in a past life, light a white candle and link into Ann who was persecuted and punished unmercifully for her witchcraft and spell craft. Once her old memories had surfaced and been dissolved, Ann developed rapidly as a psychic and medium. Ann has now opened her heart and her mind to receiving spiritual messages to help others like herself. She loves the changes that are occurring for her.

Because of her deep healing, Ann has cleared the path for you to heal those same issues right now. I have seen many people with the issue of persecution being healed and you can be healed too. Simply ask the Special Spiritual Healing Guides who deal with persecution to come forward and heal you. They have already been alerted so they are waiting for you.

Link into their powerful healing energy now, as all memories of persecution are dissolved from the deep cellular memories encoded in your DNA, your attractor fields and your physical body. It does not matter if you do not see or feel anything, the healing will still work. It just requires your prayer, courage and faith to make that decision to go forward and leave the difficult past behind.

• • •

Visitations From Spirit

Another sign you are opening psychically is that you may sense someone's presence close to you, feel someone brush your face or feel a cold shudder run all the way down your spine. This is not a physical presence. As more Spirit learn about you, word will get about and they will build their energies around you to use you as a channel. When there is a lot of Spirit around you, you might feel the temperature drop or feel someone from Spirit push you. This is usually harmless and will only affect you if you are frightened.

You could also receive messages from a grandmother or relative whom you have not seen or heard of for years. In fact you may never have met them at all. This is because Spirit do not always send us the messengers we are expecting, but instead they send the spirit guide or relative allocated to the task in hand. The family will have voted that person in after a meeting on the higher planes with your soul. Interestingly, I have suddenly become very cold as I was writing this and lost two whole lines of writing that I had to type again. Obviously someone is trying to get through to me as I write these words.

Special psychic teacher guides and spiritual Earth teachers are drafted in to help you develop when you begin to open psychically. These come and go; they are free floating spirit guides who are in service to humanity and go wherever they are needed. They receive their instructions from the higher spiritual realms.

A Visitation

Some discarnate souls can unnerve us if they feel unhappy or discontented in some way. This particularly applies to those who are still hovering close to the Earth plane for a personal reason. One very frightened woman I helped had been approached by a spiritual visitor a number of times after moving to a lovely house. During the daytime she had been quite content with her new home, but at night she had often woken to see a man at the end of her bed. She wondered what he wanted and whether she was going mad. Terrified, she called me.

I saw that this man had lived in the house some months earlier and he had been a keen gardener. He had recently died in hospital and his family had sold the house. He felt distressed that his garden had not been attended to after his death. I told her about this and that he meant her no harm. This settled her mind, for he had now become a real person with a reasonable problem. The very next day the lady began to take care of the garden and the man became happy again. If you see a ghost and it seems troubled, ask it what it needs. That way it will usually calm down. It is only there because it is unsettled in some way and because it has unfinished business. It will not harm you unless you are frightened.

There are malicious forms of spirit roaming around which attach themselves to unsuspecting victims. People who take drugs or drink excessively can fall unconscious and open themselves up to such experiences. Many spirits who have had horrendous deaths and who are still hovering above the Earth plane on the astral plane can attach themselves to these people like moths to a light. Their victim will feel very ill and uncontrollably tearful, not knowing what is wrong with them. They believe themselves to be invincible and they do not understand the dangers of falling unconscious with drugs or drink. Once the poor entities are located, lifted and removed, the person will feel better and more alive with almost four or five times as much energy. The possibility of this happening to you is virtually zero provided you take your psychic cleanses seriously.

Healing Entities

If you have been frightened by an entity, please sit down quietly and light a white candle now. Prepare yourself slowly with the powerful intent to be free of this adversity. Breathe into your heart and settle your energies. When you are ready, call upon the mighty Archangels Michael, Raphael, Ascended Master St Germain and their host of powerful angelic beings to come forward and assist you.

Place yourself inside a golden pyramid. By your side stands Archangel Raphael, the great cosmic healer. Above you is the silver blue light that will dissolve all ties as Archangel Michael descends into the golden pyramid. Carefully remove all the links coming to you from these entities with love and respect and ask that Archangel Michael removes any unseen negative energies and cuts them from you with his mighty silver blue light sword. All is dissolving in the blue-silver light, being washed away and cut at the same time. Fully acknowledge your feelings of fear as the cords are cut.

Master St Germain now appears with the huge silver ultra-violet flame of transformation that comes from the bottom of the pyramid and you are immersed in that flame. You may feel the energy around your aura moving and your third eye vibrating. Ask out loud that all attachments are cleansed, healed and transformed in the ultra-violet flames and burned to nothing. Watch as the healing takes place and wait until you feel fully calm and you know that all ties have been properly dissolved. Say, "It is done." Ask that you now receive protection at all times and thank the angels for their mighty presence and help. Allow the pyramid to dissolve from your mind.

Exorcism is not difficult. Films and television grossly exaggerate it out of all proportion.

Lights Can Flash

Sometimes lights may flash on and off when you are talking to someone here on the Earth plane. The lights are being controlled by Spirit. Things may also move and go missing only to reappear later. Kettles can switch on and off, as can televisions and computers. Light bulbs may blow too. This is Spirit trying to show you they are there.

Once when in a friend's car, we had an engine unexpectedly blow up on us on the M25 just outside London where the road merges near Croydon to make four lanes of traffic. We were suddenly stuck stationary in the fast lane. Traumatised, I looked behind me terrified that I was going to die. I saw a huge lorry flying towards us at over eighty miles an hour and I put my head between my knees ready to die – it was an odd moment. Incredibly, I then felt myself lifted up and out of the vehicle before being placed back down again. The driver, Paul, also felt the same thing although he did not tell me until some hours later. The whole episode took about four seconds.

Paul then suddenly unstrapped my safety belt and shouted, "Jump out of the car Molly and run." We jumped out of the car and both ran with all our might across all four lanes of traffic to safety. To this day I do not know how there could have been a gap in four lanes of traffic on the M25 as I have never seen that since. Shaken up, I watched from the grass verge as cars began to pile on top of one another and the police closed the motorway. Logically there was no way that the lorry rapidly speeding towards us from behind could have avoided hitting us. Spiritually we had just witnessed a miracle. I sat in a police car and heard someone from Spirit tell me to close my eyes and imagine the light of a candle flame in directly front of me at eye level. I was told to stare at it for one whole minute without thinking. I felt instantly calm.

The wrecked car belonged to a medium friend of mine, called Maggie. Upon returning to Maggie's farm some hours later in a bright yellow pick up truck, I was warmly greeted by her. I thought her calmness was rather odd considering the circumstances. She told me that Spirit had informed her of the accident and that Paul and I had sustained absolutely no mental or emotional trauma whatsoever. They had known to tell me to look at a candle because I had been practicing that method of meditation and they had removed the trauma from my memory. They had also sent a happy recovery truck driver to lift Paul's spirits and clear his trauma. The car was insured and Maggie informed us that she had decided to get rid of it anyway.

Protection for Your Journey

Before any long journey, or if you are a nervous driver, ask that the energy of your Spiritual Guardians be given to you to protect you and keep you calm. As you do this, think about my story and the immense power they have to protect and help you. Place a ring of light around your car before you leave to go anywhere.

36

More Signs of Opening Psychically

Reading Books on Angels

Perhaps you feel the urge to explore books on angels or fairies. I would recommend this as you will receive more and more help. It is the angels' Divine mission to serve you. When you ascend so do they. They love to help you and they are always in the background awaiting your call.

Angels are high spiritual beings and they are appointed by Source as angels, guides, protectors, helpers and Divine messengers. Angels have a much lighter, faster vibration than us humans which is why they cannot be seen with the naked eye.

You have a guardian angel right from birth, who stays near you throughout your life. This guardian angel will bless your marriage and if you divorce it is a good idea to hold a spiritual divorce ceremony to release the angel from its duty to you. There are small angels and large angels who have bigger tasks to perform. Angels create Divine celestial music and have been seen by mystics and spiritual masters throughout history. They are flocking to the Earth right now in their millions to help us raise our consciousness.

I have asked the angels to come forward to assist in many of the healings which are included in this book as I know the strength and power they bring. I have seen the results of their miracle-working many times.

As you progress psychically and your awareness heightens, you may become sensitive to hurting even the tiniest creature. Aysha, a young Asian woman who loves flowers, began to purchase organic slug pellets so that the slugs could be stunned and simply moved rather than killed. Diana, a spiritual friend of mine who writes beautiful books on angels, painstakingly removed every slug in her garden by hand one summer. At the time I considered her behaviour as very strange as I had not yet sufficiently evolved to understand the non-harming of everything, including the tiniest of God's creatures. Nowadays I would probably do the same.

A Song Can Be Played Over and Over

Sometimes you may hear a song being played over and over in your mind. If this happens, notice the words or the title. What are the angels trying to say to you? Julie, a promising young psychic from central London, told me that her father in spirit, who often came close, always played her a certain tune before his arrival.

Colours Have More Meaning

You may be more drawn to a particular colour or colours. Beautiful pale pinks, mauves and turquoises spring to mind, or deeper violet hues. They all mean something. I remember going through a mad pink phrase and when I opened my wardrobe it was totally girlie – there was pink everywhere! I had pink bath salts, pink soap, pink toilet paper, a pink wash bag, pink flowers in the garden, pink socks. I even had pink sheets on the bed top and bottom. "This is getting ridiculous," I thought, as I began searching for a pink laptop. I knew pink was linked to love and partnerships and that it reduced anger in others, but I had not realised that it is also good for group work and issues of self-acceptance. At the time I had just started teaching groups and I needed to boost my confidence. Unknowingly, I had chosen so many pink things to bond the groups and raise my self-esteem.

If you love eating salt and have had to lower its intake for health reasons, then try Himalayan pink crystal salt as a substitute as it is excellent for your health. It is a lovely colour, totally pure and it contains every known mineral and trace element in your body. You can eat it and rest assured that it is doing you good. The pink crystal chunks also make excellent bath companions and they are useful for cleansing your aura and purifying the bath water.

Urgent Psychic Messages

As you grow psychically you might get a sudden "urge" to tell someone something that you think will benefit them. These messages can feel urgent and they are usually felt in the solar plexus and do not go away unless they are expressed. This is because the spirit sending you the message feels a sense of worry or urgency.

I once received a message of this nature to warn a young woman called to have a breast cancer scan. Spirit told me she would develop cancer eight years in the future. I could also see it in her aura as a slight mound, brownish in colour and heavier than the energy around it. Sadly, she laughed it off, informing me that no one could possibly know something that far in advance.

Nowadays, modern science is finding that these illnesses manifest deep inside the energy field of the person years before they manifest physically. In fact they are discovering that all physical illness is primarily energy based.

A Healing For Cancer

If you have cancer, link into the energy that I will send over to you now to help heal this. Sit quietly and feel this powerful force field come straight to the cancerous spot. Ask the powerful spirit guides from the higher realms especially responsible for healing cancer to come forward. Ask out loud that the deeper inner meaning of why this has been created in your body is shown to you. Ask out loud and with reverence that it is cleared. The powerful psychic and energy healing is now being sent to you.

Place the palm of your hand at the back of your head, the thumb of the other hand on the inside of your eye just below your eyebrow and your ring finger in the same way next to the other eye, to heal and dissolve the energies around this situation. Keep your hands in place as you think about the situation until you feel the energy move.

See it as an energy block only that your body can heal, for that is what it is. If your body made it, it can also heal it.

A friend of mine went through six months of chemo without sickness or fatigue. She managed this via the incredible help given to her by asking her spirit guides to bolster her energy and clear her expectation that she would suffer. Ultimately she did not suffer. Because of her commitment and deep trust, Spirit immediately rallied round to help her heal.

Aches and Pain From Spirit

Have you ever seen a medium on stage suddenly bend over as if they are in pain? Often, as this happens, they describe the illness of the person who is trying to speak through them. When opening psychically it is quite possible to take on the pain of a discarnate soul especially if they died an uncomfortable death. They may also have had ailments when they were alive. You could suddenly find yourself with a chronic backache or a feeling of depression as they try to communicate with you.

You can be taught not to do this and healing can be brought in so that you only respond neutrally. If you are clairsentient and feel things deeply, you may pick up diverse energies around people who are alive. It is important to learn how to rid yourself of adverse energies that could pass through your body. Constantly cleansing the aura and the energy in and around your body is essential to keep you well. In addition, become aware of how you relate to that particular person or their pain. This in itself may need healing. Check your beliefs too. Do you believe you have to attract their pain to heal them?

Healing Another's Pain

If you have taken on another's pain, (even the pain from your ancestors) ask out loud for their guardian angel to be brought forward to heal them and that you are disconnected from their pain. Ask that their pain is dissolved and that love is brought to them. If you are very sensitive you may see images of this taking place. Lights can bounce around the person, or you might see the colour and brightness of their aura change.

If the pain is in your body rub the spot gently and point this out to Archangel Raphael for a thorough clearance and healing.

Out of Body Experiences

I have met a number of people who have had out of body experiences. Rosie springs to mind. She had lost her partner suddenly in an accident on a mountain in Bulgaria. This started a flow of people dying all around her; workmates, relatives, friends and even animals. It did not stop for five years or more. Emotionally exhausted, her health began to deteriorate and one of her lungs collapsed. Rosie was rushed into hospital and clearly remembers falling unconscious. She told me that she entered a beautiful light tunnel and felt unbelievably well.

She was met by a spirit guide who told her she could pass on if she so wished. But Rosie suddenly realised that her sister would be devastated so she chose to return to her body back on the Earth plane. Whenever she tells this story to me she explains how amazing the bright lights were and the beauty of the spirit guides. She says that her experience of the lights was totally incomparable to the dimension that we live in for they were truly magical.

Floating Out At Night

I have often floated out at night, fully aware that I am healing somewhere. People ring me and tell me they have seen me hovering over them at night, healing and amending their problems.

It could be that you are doing the same without even realising it. Some people say they grow tired if they leave their bodies to astral travel. I have never found this to be true. If you wish to do healing work on the inner planes at night, ensure you place a strong protection field around your aura before you go to sleep. You can also ask that you travel to the light dwellings of the ascended masters and angels to rest with them at night.

A true out of body experience is totally different from anything else you may know, as you literally leave your body. I have had an out of body experience, completely aware that I did not have a body and that I was someplace which was full of strange phenomena. I saw alien creatures that were half human and strange landscapes that I have never experienced here. I believe this was the lower astral plane. I was also aware that a huge mass of energy had rushed out of the top of my head just before this happened. During the experience the images lightened so I observed that I had travelled to the higher astral planes. I could not describe this out of body experience at all. Even floating would have implied that I was doing something, but I was not. I just "was." I could only observe and not think. I had no feelings whatsoever, only observations. I could not control when the experience began, nor when it would end. I did not know that it would begin or end either.

The following day I lectured students at the local college and some of them broke down in tears because the energy projected from my solar plexus was so strong. It was like a powerful laser beam and they could see and feel its intensity. They said it was warm and bright. I have seen this only once in my lifetime coming from a lady spiritual teacher who had spent months meditating with the gurus in India. She was a teacher of rebirthing.

Directly after this, I received large sums of money in the post completely out of the blue.

Sacred Places

Another sign of opening psychically and spiritually is the need to visit sacred places. One couple who recently came to see me knew they had to be together the moment they saw each other. Recently they had been travelling around the world together visiting the sacred chakras of the planet without realising the significance. They had visited the Pyramids in Egypt, Glastonbury in England and Macchu Picchu, all in just under a year. They had thought it odd that they were spending so much time and money abroad and they felt concerned that they might travel the entire world and deplete all their finances before the urge died down.

On their return, however, they were able to heal others and psychically guide them. Without their knowledge, their souls had taken them on a spiritual journey and shown them how to channel and pass on the secrets of ancient psychic knowledge. They are now in the process of setting up a healing centre in Devon.

A Healing Prayer for Direction and Financial Help

Take a moment and link into Mark and Rose's love for one another. Sense their calm, spiritual energy. When you do this, you will receive the deep healing they experienced, which completely turned their lives around. Mark and Rose received confirmation of their direction and a path opened to move forward and leave their old lives behind. They instinctively knew they would be guided, financially safe and protected by their spiritual guardians.

If you need direction, finances and help with the unfolding of your path, pray that you will be guided and that you will receive financial help. Ask Lakshmi the Hindu Goddess of Wealth and Prosperity to draw near. Ask that your lack of faith about being safe is lifted from you and replaced with trust. Ask that any deep-seated fear is lifted and healed and that any past lives and recent karma to do with money are dissolved.

37

Are You Happy Being Psychic Or Not?

Feeling happy about being psychic is a delicate matter, as being subjected to so much unseen information can be quite a responsibility and set you apart from the mainstream. If you feel comfortable about developing psychically and know that you are here to do so, keep going. If people around you are uncomfortable with this, you may just have to let them be so. If you want to attend workshops just for the fun of it, that is a very good reason for doing so. If this applies to you, go ahead, have fun and you may or may not find that you develop. Keep it light and easy.

If you want your energy to lighten and you sometimes battle with seriousness or a heavy approach to psychic matters, read books on the elementals. They will come to you and bring the light, fun-loving and mischievous energies of the divas, fairies and Earth spirits. Make friends with Irish people too as they are good with the elementals. I was fascinated by the Irish people's ability to discuss the fairies living at the bottom of their gardens. For them this is completely normal so why do we think otherwise? The Irish also have open hearts – an essential for communicating with those little diva souls.

Spend more time with others who understand your need for spirituality and the psychic world. You are certainly not alone. If you feel you are, get some healing for loneliness to clear the blocks and then your new psychic friends will arrive.

With all this psychic development and the changes taking place in your life, what do you think you are learning spiritually and why? Have you ever thought about this very important question? It is certain that your soul is broadcasting messages and wanting you to grow. This can feel frustrating sometimes, especially if you have been reluctant to listen.

Your Soul Wants to Grow and Expand

Frances, who had been studying to be a psychic for two years, had one such experience. After many years of being happily married, her husband suddenly became attracted to a woman twenty years his junior. Frances was distraught and angry. She felt she had been a good wife and a devoted mother. What she did not know was that her soul wanted to grow and expand, not only psychically but spiritually too. It wanted her to develop courage.

During a psychic reading I saw that Frances had lost a child in a past life in England during Victorian times. She had excess milk and so became a nursemaid to a family feeding their baby as part of her duties. She was heartbroken, physically exhausted and hurt. One cold November morning in the mid 1800's, she bitterly cried out in pain making a pact with herself and God that she would put up with anything to have a child.

Many years later – but in another lifetime – it happened. Frances had unknowingly built up a strong cloud of psychic energy on the astral with her intense desire; a desire so strong that it could not be extinguished and it had to be fulfilled in another lifetime. The pact came to pass. She had a very naughty daughter who was defiant and difficult and who repeatedly forced her to go against her gentle nature, rise up and become stronger.

Her husband's affair also forced her to confront the other woman and face her inner fears of being unable to express herself. Frances faced up to her husband, ended the affair and found she could now express her psychic potential as her throat chakra had unblocked. This took a great deal of courage. She faced losing her husband and overturning her restricted reserved *background and the pain of the past. Frances sensed she was being guided as she had booked an appointment to see me about something completely different. This all blew up in her face the night before we met.*

Now that her throat chakra was nicely open, she began to channel wonderful uplifting messages of courage to others. I was told her child would now develop her own expressive personality that had been suppressed and that she would later become a journalist. The two of them had agreed to aid one another during this lifetime.

Fear of Speaking Up

If you are to become a medium or psychic you will need to be able to speak your truth. If you are afraid of confronting people, fearful of the backlash, or feel stuck, you will need to heal. If you cannot speak properly and you are self-conscious about your ability to talk to others, sit quietly and link into Frances and her courage. You will receive healing from Spirit. It may feel a little strange when the healing flows through your body. I am also sending healing to open your throat chakra now.

• • •

Psychic Sabotage

We have just spent some time discussing your psychic development, but what if you are progressing the way you wish to and then it all suddenly goes wrong? Psychic sabotage is when you encourage something to block you from going forward. Your subconscious may not agree with what you want for yourself and may stop you from progressing further. You could also doubt your own ability, doubt your intuition, or pay too much attention to disbelievers around you. You will soon find out who you can tell about your psychic ability and who you cannot. If you were to enlighten me about any difficulties you have relating to others' opinions, I would advise you to keep your own counsel. You do not have to convince anyone about your interest in psychic matters and you do not need to tell everyone about your perceptions or your gifts. If you do, there will be a need in you either to convince them or to reassure yourself. This need is better off being dissolved and healed.

Even though you may be the most confident of people, you might still be influenced by another's opinion, especially if you value that person highly and they are important to you. All this wastes your valuable time, which you could be using to develop yourself.

I know this is not easy, but try and accept the pace you are developing at. Graham wanted constant proof and he craved the end goal without enjoying the journey. Rayno consistently asked me how long it would take him to become fully psychic, but it does not work like that. You cannot force the pace. I asked them both to slow down. Impatience will definitely chase away the subtle psychic energies you might otherwise observe. Overcoming that impatience may be a part of your soul's challenge.

It is also possible that you might not even notice how much you are improving, unless you are keeping a diary, which is highly recommended. The chances are that someone close to you will notice far more than you do. Developing psychically can take a lifetime and most of the good mediums and psychics I know have many years of development and practice under their belt.

Graham's Story

Graham craved the ability to see clairvoyantly. In psychic development classes most of the other students were having clairvoyant experiences apart from him.

When we spoke I received a psychic impression that this had also happened in school when he was younger, which transpired to be true. A memory suddenly sprang to Graham's mind of being humiliated in front of the entire class. I also knew that he was a feeling type of person, a clairsentient and not prone to thinking predominately in pictures. Graham would most likely get impressions in his body before seeing pictures. I explained this over and over again to Graham, but I knew I was not getting through. The longer it took and the more Graham ached for some kind of "seeing experience" the more he blocked it.

Graham always sprang to life when we did something physical. I realised that to develop psychically he needed to develop his body experiences.

On a soft green lawn, one warm Sunday afternoon at a psychic development workshop, I tried another way in. I demonstrated the power of the Higher Self by using my body in front of the class. I showed them how they could bring energy through from their higher selves and how my Higher Self could give me another five inches of flexibility. I certainly could not do this on my own. They were all spellbound, except for skeptic Graham who badly needed proof. I sensed that Spirit were about to "pull something out of the bag" and he was about to get it. I gently said, "Go ahead Graham, if you don't believe what you have just seen, have a go yourself. Do the same as I have just done and speak to your Higher Self."

Graham, in a loud demanding voice, suddenly called out to his Higher Self and commanded, "If you exist, move my body in such a way that I'll definitely know you are there." Graham was instantly taken over by his Higher Self and he was thrown to the grass, landing flat on his face. Fortunately he was very fit, but his Higher Self knew this. I remember the group being completely overwhelmed by the whole spectacle and the force of the fall. Graham, although still trying to doubt it because he had not seen a clairvoyant vision, had undergone an experience that he simply could not deny. Graham also finally realised that he had been consumed with the idea that he "needed to become a clairvoyant." The need was too intense. At last he understood and allowed the healing energies through and so the intensity was healed and Graham reached a neutral state. The psychic impressions and knowings began to emerge at that point because now they could. Graham had always been a powerful healer but he had never known why. Now he is able to accept that this is the case and he still does not consciously know how.

Graham was rearing a young family. A sudden change in his career would have been financially devastating for his two young sons and incredibly stressful for his wife. It was not the right time.

Healing Impatience for Psychic Gifts

If you crave psychic ability it can sometimes be held up. The very craving means the desire is too strong. Spirit usually only work with those who are calm and detached about the outcome. Craving a psychic ability is ego-based. Although this is not wrong, there is usually some unconscious anxiety accompanying this that needs to go.

Sit quietly and ask that your need for psychic ability be lifted from you. Forcing the issue will just not work as it will only serve to do the opposite and chase away any potential psychic talent you may have. Ask out loud that powerful healing energies accompany your request and that your Higher Self removes this craving for you and it will do so. You will still receive psychic gifts but the intense need for them will be lifted.

38

Dealing With Change

A Lack of Purpose

You could be feeling a distinct lack of purpose, like a ship without a rudder. It can feel frightening, disturbing and disorientating. If this is happening to you, please recognise that it is a common side-effect of developing spiritually. Thank goodness it is only a temporary state. It is important to talk to someone if you can – preferably someone who is either also going through this themselves or who has already done so. You may also feel isolated and cut off from others. There were times when I was moving from one psychic or spiritual frequency to another so often that I felt totally isolated; I was releasing memories of being in an incubator as a baby and of being totally alone. In reality, I was leaving practically everyone I knew behind. It felt scary, isolating and the loneliness was overwhelming.

I also felt I had nothing in common with my family members who seemed to be living in another world. Since then many of the people have reappeared in my life after I was able to reach a neutral state about them. Many people on a spiritual path have incarnated into families that do not understand their spiritual views or who label them as odd. You may even feel that you cannot stay with your family because of their approach to life. As you progress, the idea of non-harming others becomes more relevant and sometimes we must simply understand that our families are on a different level of consciousness. This can be difficult and I have known a number of psychics who have had to rise above these challenges. It is said that we choose our families to grow and work out karma,

189

so what you are experiencing is a part of that plan even if it feels uncomfortable.

During my own "alone phase," even on warm sunny summer days, a terrible depression engulfed me, only lifting at evening time. I could not attribute it to the weather as the sun was shining brightly. At the time I did not know that my soul had chosen to go through a deep purification. Layer upon layer of energy was being cleared throughout the day leaving me feeling much better by the evening. When the energy became stuck it felt extremely uncomfortable and often I would need healing from another. Each morning began with uncontrollable anxiety that went on for hours. Spirit, however, always sent someone in to help and I have always been supported through my changes.

If you are experiencing "down" moods, do not be afraid to admit what might be taking place for you and ask for help. We are all here to support one another and lift one another up through dark times.

Healing Depression for a Lack of Purpose

If you want to be psychic but feel a lack of purpose and have bouts of depression or intense fear, then acknowledge your emotions. You are experiencing an energy block in your body caused by stuck emotion. Ask out loud that Archangel Raphael comes forward with his host of powerful healing angels to heal you and ask that Mary, Queen of the Angels, accompanies him.

Light a candle and pray hard for the depression to start moving. Pray for your purpose to be shown to you and keep praying until something changes.

Wait quietly while the healing takes place. Allow any emotions to come up from inside and feel them leave. You may see the depression as a shape, a colour, a word or a heavy feeling. Keep praying.

Breathe in deeply so you fill your lungs right up. As you breathe out, send the negative emotion out of your body and into the atmosphere. Notice what it looks and feels like and experience it leaving. Watch as St Raphael's healing angels dissolve it safely for you.

Vigorous exercise also shifts stuck energy. Go running, swimming, or exercise until you get out of breath.

People Will Come and Go

People always come and go in our lives but when we develop psychically they tend to come and go even more quickly. This rapid turnover can feel quite alarming. Some people, even close friends or lovers, are likely to leave your life quickly the moment you dissolve and heal the pattern that was joining you.

Life may begin to throw more and more at you to deal with the changes and it could feel like you are on a speeding rollercoaster.

> *An exhausted Patsy came to see me one sunny Monday afternoon as her son had stormed out of the house and had not spoken to her since the previous Wednesday. Then her horse suddenly died at 5.30pm on the Friday even though he had been well in the morning. She damaged her van on the Saturday, her partner had six punctures in a month and her father was ill, arguing with her mother, whose new partner suddenly refused to have him around. Wearily, she asked me, "What on Earth is going on?" Spirit told me she was repaying monetary karma and being asked to stand up for herself. Her journey was difficult and tiring, but it was nearly over.*

It is easy for me to tell you that you are fine and safe if, like Patsy, you are also living through a great amount of change. Embrace every emotion and let it run through you and heal you. That way you will keep up with the frequency fluctuations.

The Earth is now changing rapidly and all those predictions about the land shifts and floods are coming true – although it is now known that if enough people pray to stop the upheaval it will subside. As this pace quickens we will need to let go of all the issues that have stopped us from being the powerful human beings we can become. Your body is also changing with the flood of new cosmic energies coming to the Earth at this time and your psychic chakras are gradually opening and spinning more efficiently. Periodically you may feel a drawing feeling around the forehead as your third eye stretches to open up more. This is normal.

You Are Burning Karma

Please remember that your emotional body is cleansing thousands of years of karma and burning it away. This is an incredible process. As you open psychically and each time the Earth's consciousness takes an energy shift – especially during eclipses and planetary astrological line-ups – you are releasing deep-seated negative blocks that have previously stopped you from moving forward. Circumstances and people will come in to evoke those changes whether you like it or not. Try to recognise what they are mirroring in you and get healing as often as you can.

If all of this is overwhelming to you, you could try to slow the process down and take some time out. Rest as much as possible and go out in the daylight. Make sure you exercise and get out of breath. A brisk walk is perfect as it shifts stuck energy. You made your soul contract before incarnating and if you chose a huge change or a lot of challenges, sooner or later you will need to live them, as this is karmic law. If this applies to you and you sometimes feel as if you are floundering, I have asked for healing and energy to help and sustain you.

Taking Time Out

During my development, I have found it necessary to stray from my path from time to time. For nearly two years I studied Neuro-Linguistic Programming (NLP) and worked with top sportsmen, leaving the psychic work behind. I vividly remember the day I stood up in a luxurious golf club talking about winning. After the talk, I stepped down from the stage and knew that I would remove my brogues and mid-calf skirt and never talk about the mental side of golf again. The karma was complete.

When I look back over this period of my life I can now see that it was a necessary karmic unveiling. You may find you need to take a break from developing psychically and this is fine. It is all about balance and the need to work along your pathway in order to fit in with your life. It is no good taking a year out to meditate if you have not got enough money. Perhaps your soul is asking you to address this issue before taking the step. I once knew a man who did just this and when he returned to England he found it very difficult to adjust to living here again.

Taking time out, although essential, may mean that the events happen somewhere else instead.

Ann, a psychic animal communicator from Hertfordshire, had a wonderful way with animals. Ann, like Patsy, had been going through a lot of changes in her life and she thought that travelling to Tibet would help her to overcome the traumas and dramas. She was convinced that sitting in a Tibetan temple would help to cure her weight problem, her arthritis and her hurting kidney. She was really looking forward to going to Tibet and had saved up for over a year.

Ann has always been grounded and not prone to hallucinations. She had consulted a psychic medium and an astrologer before travelling and they both confirmed that this would be the end of a long and difficult life journey for her. I felt less sure but I did not wish to spoil her enthusiasm.

Once she arrived in Tibet she had to endure the climbing of many steep hills. Her overweight body could not cope with the climbing and her heart could not deal with the high altitudes. She tried hard, but she simply could not make the climbs. The local Tibetans laughed at Ann and their behaviour smashed her fantasy of a perfect Tibet. She realised they were people with limitations just like anyone else. Ann was singled out and humiliated. In tears she told me how she had seen pictures of past lives when she had been publicly humiliated at her own hanging. All of these feelings of humiliation had to go. Her soul wanted her to be free. It had taken her all the way to Tibet to connect her with those very souls whose job it was to bring these old wounds to the surface.

When she got back she lost her job, something that had never happened before. Her soul was cleansing and releasing the need to feel in or out of control. After a deep healing Ann became calm and neutral. She had wanted to become an animal healer and needed her psychic ability to read the animals. She had delayed starting this new venture for just a bit too long and because of this Ann got a rude, spiritual wake up call to get on with it.

Healing Procrastination

If you are delaying working with your psychic or spiritual abilities, please accept this healing of courage and opening for you to begin to do the work you incarnated to complete.

I am asking Spirit to send you love, support and a deep healing to pave the way for the changes within you to occur. Sit quietly whilst this happens. Now think about what doubts are holding you up. While this healing takes place you can sip a hot drink.

Fears Can Intensify

You may fear loss or lack of money, and this can be very intense. Like Georgina, you may dread losing people you love and need. You may even fear losing your sanity (this can usually be traced back to a past life where you were in some kind of asylum.) You could also fear being out of control. I once experienced this when a past life memory came up about being a servant. I had visited a stately home that contained a lot of Victorian furniture. When I aspired to rise above that station this time and expand further than my parents, my ancestors began to come though in their droves because it was all too much for them. I needed to release their limitations.

Amidst all of these changes you might also feel as if you have been chosen for something really special. Why else would you be going through such great change? You might even be trying to help everyone you meet, only to feel hurt or rejected when some of them refuse you. Perhaps in your own loving rush to "help and save" you did not notice that they were not asking for help. They may even see it as interference which could feel even more exasperating or hurtful.

Do You Need to Save Others?

I find that people who run what I call a "saviour pattern" do so because they feel a certain level of guilt about not having done enough, either for one or both of their parents or in a previous existence. It can also go back to something they have done but that they cannot forgive themselves for. This "something" may well be unconscious and unknown to them and it is very common in psychics and mediums. They can feel they have done something very wrong somewhere in the past but often they do not know what. As a result they often feel undeserving.

Ruth would always give strangers snippets of psychic information; people on buses, tubes, planes—wherever

195

she found herself. She was especially interested in dogs and would walk her own dogs in the woods and local quarry giving psychic messages to dog owners, which she picked up from their animals. Very often she was right. People were polite to her, so for a long time Ruth carried on giving these messages not realising that she was not always taken seriously.

One day Ruth joined a psychic circle and in her usual bubbly way she began to channel psychic messages for everyone present. Some of the members became uneasy, agitated and irritated. Her messages fell on stony ground even though they were accurate, interesting and well meant. She felt naturally upset and could not understand where she had gone wrong. From her perspective she was only trying to help and give these people love from their animals.

In her childhood Ruth had not been believed or taken seriously when she channelled from spirit. Her subconscious was still holding onto the hurt and because of this the same thing was happening all over again years down the line. Ruth had a psychic healing and her subconscious let go of the past. Her messages were accepted from that day onwards. Ruth also learned to use her intuition to assess whether or not it was appropriate to give a message. Once her pattern of not being taken seriously had been cleared, she received a lot of thanks and appreciation from people.

If you feel you are not acknowledged when you are helping others, let us heal this now. If you are going to be a psychic or a healer you will need to be taken seriously with all the messages you give. What would be the point otherwise? Ruth was completely healed and she is now respected by many for her incredible psychic talents.

Healing Lack of Acknowledgement

Being acknowledged is essential for all of us and especially important for a developing psychic. If you are not taken seriously, ask yourself where you have not thought that another's opinion was important. Perhaps you did not want to hear what they had to say or perhaps they criticised you. You may have been constantly criticised in childhood. You might not have been acknowledged or listened to or your self-esteem may be too low to even expect people to listen to you.

As you sit quietly reading and thinking about this, I am asking your spiritual guardians to draw close to you to directly pick up on your energy and send you lots of healing. You may have realisations whilst this takes place. This healing will encourage others to treat you with respect in the future. Make a pact with yourself that you will also listen to another person and give 100 per cent of your attention next time someone has anything to say to you.

Logic Versus Intuition

There will be times when you are not sure about what you are receiving in the way of a message either for yourself or another. The logical mind constantly needs reassurance as you begin to develop psychically so it can recognise and accept the psychic information coming through.

One young man from South Africa had spent most of his life worrying about making a mistake. He had done this at school back home, as well as in business and he felt amazed that it was holding him up from becoming a really good psychic. He was certainly receiving a lot of input from Spirit but he was afraid to use it for fear of being wrong. His intuition would say one thing and his logical mind another. I asked him to imagine moving his brain from his head down into his stomach and make a decision from there. We also did a psychic healing session where he regressed to his school days to all the times he had been picked on by the teachers, who bullied pupils unmercifully if they made mistakes. Interestingly, the teachers were also terrified of making a mistake in case they lost their jobs.

In that school making a mistake meant punishment. It meant shame, detention and a letter home to your parents. Once this psychic block had been emotionally cleared, he was able to listen to his intuition and allow Spirit through.

It may sometimes seem like there is a little person inside of you gleefully waiting to tell you that you might be "wrong" in some of the messages you bring through. None of us are perfect. This worry can occur when someone sitting in front of you desperately wants a different outcome to their reading. They could be pressurising you. If this happens, stop, come away from them and leave the room if you have to. Once you are outside, do a quick aura clearance, centre yourself and return refreshed so you can sense the answer. Come out of your mind, put your consciousness in your middle and sense or feel if what you are receiving is true. Ask yourself, "Does this feel right?"

Hand it Over to Spirit

If after all that you are still not sure, hand it over to Spirit and ask them out loud for the answer. You could do this in front of your enquirer and tell him or her what you are doing. This way you are taking yourself out of the equation and handing over the responsibility to Spirit. Nine times out of ten Spirit will come up trumps and respond – usually with an answer which is not at all what you are expecting and which can be a startling revelation to both of you. When you do this, you may have to wait a moment for their reply and to a beginner this time lapse can seem interminable. Spirit occasionally need to go and find the right spiritual guardian for that particular message.

On the odd occasion when no reply is forthcoming, please say so. Never second-guess something because you fear not knowing and you are worried about your reputation. Your reputation as a good psychic will be built on honesty. We are not always given the answer because we are not always meant to know it ahead of time. This is especially true of situations where karma is involved. I have seen this occur on numerous occasions.

Obsession

I once met a vibrant, pretty lady who wanted a relationship with a man who periodically flitted in and out of her life. He always had another woman in the background and was running a series of unfulfilled relationships. She had waited for this man for twenty years. Their on-off relationship went on for six years until she finally reached a point at which the pain became too unbearable and she wanted to let go.

The two people in question had been through many past lives where they had separated time and again. She had always stayed in the relationship because she had thought that to resolve all of these separations they would need to clear all of the past lives and then be together. She had also been his slave so she had unconsciously succumbed to his wishes in several of those lifetimes.

Her path in this lifetime was to complete her karma and overcome being out of control emotionally and take back her power. However, such was her desire for this man that she spent huge sums of money and had more than fifty readings in her search for someone to tell her that she would be with him.

Forty-nine psychics did just that and told her she would be with him. Only one went to Spirit who consulted the Akashic Records and told her otherwise.

At a deep level the woman knew this information was true but she was angry with the one medium who had got it right. Unconsciously she had been ready to hear the truth or she would not have found that medium, however, consciously she still fought the truth with her anger. Each and every one of those readers had been right at that moment, but they had felt overwhelmed by her desperation and although many of them had used the tarot, they had not given her a correct long term reading.

This happened because karmic veils were in place and she was not allowed to know the real outcome until she was ready to leave the man. The psychics and mediums were giving her a reading based on telepathy, based on the knowledge of her past so far. The tarot cards gave the possible outcome to keep her in the relationship until she had learned the karmic lesson her soul wanted her to learn, which was to put herself first, respect herself and leave him.

Had the first psychic told her this, she would not have accepted it because she was not ready and that is why she continued searching. She was not ready to have the karma removed. When she was told she would be with him, she did not believe this either and that is why she went on having more and more readings. Unconsciously she knew she would not stay with this man. The one medium who remained neutral and handed it over to Spirit, got it right

I am telling you this story so you understand the enormous power Spirit has to back you once you trust. The one medium who "got it right" did so because of her belief system in her own accuracy and her trust in her spirit guides and because the timing was right. All the others also "got it right" for the timing of the reading and the evolution of the two people involved.

39

Psychic Requirements

Sunshine and Light

You may crave light and sunshine and feel the need to go to sunnier climates more often. If you cannot do this, it might be a good idea to purchase a "light box" to bring more light into your home, especially during the winter months. You may notice and smell traffic fumes much more readily than before. You could be more aware of conserving nature and notice other people's pollution and their lack of interest in keeping their space orderly or their immediate environment clean. You could notice yourself becoming more orderly and discarding things as soon as you do not need them.

The old structures that exist in the way of your job, your marriage, your family, and your environment may start crumbling around you. It could also be that you are craving change and instigating it, even though it might be a scary thing to do. Many psychic students do not know why they crave change, but these changes are a natural extension of any internal changes taking place within as you develop.

If you have elected to live a simple straightforward life you may not experience too much external change. This will largely depend upon the spiritual contracts you have made before incarnating.

Gaining Psychic Confidence

I have never yet met anyone developing psychically who was completely confident of their ability. This is because some of your experiences are so unlike anything you have ever experienced before. You will not be able to use your logical or conscious mind to find out how or why things happen in the psychic realms. Psychic experiences do not live in this part of your mind. They live in the ethers. Moreover, did you know that your conscious mind, which is the part of your mind that plans your day, thinks about making a meal and getting jobs done, only makes up a tiny four per cent of who you are? That leaves a whopping 96 per cent of your mind power which is consciously unaccountable for.

You may have searched in vain for answers to your psychic questions. This is because you have searched in your conscious mind where there are no answers.

Frances had no idea that she had lost a child in a previous lifetime, nor that she had not stood up for herself. She did not know that her unconscious was still acting out these past life events because it had not been shown otherwise. She had no idea that she had carried this energy through from her previous lifetime in order to grow spiritually. She only knew that she thought her partner was having an affair and that she felt angry and hurt. Her emotions and her conscious memory were only symptoms of the unconscious source of the problem. Once she had accessed the past life creating it, experienced it in her body and released it, her emotions and her conscious mind calmed down.

Train Your Mind to Meditate

To become a psychic, you will need to be able to distinguish between when Spirit is "speaking to you" and when your own mind is chattering, whether what you are seeing is actually "real" or a mind fabrication. You may find it difficult to be still at first, so a meditation built on watching your thoughts will encourage you to relax.

To practice this, you will need to sit still and watch what is taking place in your mind. You can stop and start the thoughts at random and watch them come and go. If you begin to have feelings, you have got involved with the thought flow and you need to come out again and become the observer. If you learn to meditate you will learn more quickly, breathe more easily and you will be healthier and more resilient. You will even look younger and definitely develop more rapidly as a psychic. In my home study psychic workbook, I cover meditation in much greater detail.

Meditation is the basis of your psychic ability. Sometimes you may not feel that you are doing it right, but keep going, as in a few weeks this will be a thing of the past. The best form of meditation is to watch the breath and allow your mind to follow it as it comes in and out of your body. As you continue to watch and listen to the sound of the breath it will shorten and open up more cosmic energy to flood in through your crown chakra, for distribution through the etheric around your body and its seventy-two thousand psychic passages. Remember, if thoughts come in, watch them and do not give them energy. If you hear yourself saying, "I am not thinking anything," you are still thinking or else you will not have heard that thought.

The first time I successfully meditated, I felt my entire mind had been cleaned out. It was as if I had been on holiday and I was totally rested and refreshed. Meditate daily and you will gain access to that altered state of consciousness, which is necessary for you to become psychic. Do not skip this part of your training as it is vital.

If you are active by nature, you could find that exercise can become a meditation. If you like drinking coffee, make that your meditation and enjoy every sip, tasting it with absolute pleasure.

If you wish to develop psychically, train your conscious mind to keep impressing upon your unconscious that you wish to move in this direction. In your thoughts think about how you would be if you were an accurate psychic. What would you be doing? Where would you be? Who would you spend time with? How would you dress? Talk to yourself with your inner voice too. What would you say to people? How would they listen to what you have to say? You can also "feel" how it would be if you were as psychic as you wish. Would you feel proud of yourself? Or satisfied?

This kind of thinking and daydreaming makes something happen in your unconscious because it is being shown something in a way it can understand. Once your subconscious accepts something, it will move Heaven and Earth to make it happen for you. When you can "feel" something, you are already there. You are instantly aligning with its magnetic field and you only have to draw it to you in order to manifest it. Feeling that you already have it is an important part of the process.

Think about this for a moment. Whenever something has happened to you that you have wanted badly you have spent time planning and thinking about it beforehand. Girls spend ages planning their weddings. They love dreaming about the wonderful dress they will wear on their special day.

You have probably spent time thinking about and planning holidays which you want to go on or luxury items you want to buy. You enjoyed thinking about all of this. When I knew that I wanted to expand my business via the internet, I thought about it and worked it out in my mind. I thought about the cost, the wording and seeing the name of my psychic school at the top of Google. I mentally planned the website and the colours and I even worked out who would come to see me, who would ring me and so on. I thought about working with clients on Skype whilst I enjoyed the sun in Spain during winter as Britain froze. I was daydreaming and mind-planning even though I was not aware of this. I did not sit down and say, "Now I am going to visualise," although you can always set time aside to do that. It is just that I was already visualising, using my brain and mind the way I always do when I want something. I just kept thinking about it.

Finding the Answers From Within

Your conscious mind is perpetually questioning. This is its job and it can be tiring. Questions such as, "Why am I psychic?" "Am I special?" "Why isn't this happening to my friends?" "Why aren't they emotional?" "Why don't they feel the need to help people?" "Why is all this negativity coming up from my past?" and "Why is my life so challenging when theirs is so easy?" are just a few that I hear on a daily basis. To develop psychically you will need a quieter mind. This is not an easy feat with all the internal changes that you will go through. To answer all your questions and quell the mental busyness, you need to access your unconscious mind.

Your unconscious mind is fascinating; a huge reservoir of ancient and modern knowledge. It also has entry to an even more elite field of "psychic knowing" called the "collective unconscious." This is where you operate through telepathy and, for instance, if you think about someone they ring you. It is where the thoughts, ideas, intentions and past, present and future of every single living being are held, including animals, plants, trees, stones, etc. The quicker you can access your subconscious, the better psychic you will become. Trying to make things happen is the domain of the conscious mind. Allowing things to unfold is the domain of the unconscious.

Your conscious mind needs to be trained to ask the unconscious for the answers to your questions. It also needs to be trained to de-clutter, as a constant whirling of pointless thoughts going round and round in your mind will certainly get in the way of any psychic knowledge coming through. At night, or as you awaken in a semi-conscious state, ask your unconscious to come up with an answer or start to make things happen for you. You can ask your unconscious to remove old patterns and heal you. It is especially prone to accepting commands when you are about to fall asleep, just waking up, or in a state of hypnotic trance.

When you have asked your question, a thought usually randomly pops up in your mind when you least expect it; a bit like when you cannot remember someone's name. You may go through the alphabet in your mind hoping to be prompted by a letter at the beginning of their name. You may also hope that they have not noticed you are only calling them "you" for the entire time you were with them. The next day, however, when you do not need to know anymore, or it is not important, their name suddenly pops up in your mind. This is how it works and sometimes the answers will come quicker than others. The less you care about the answer, the more readily the subconscious delivers the information. This is because the energies are relaxed.

I think the act of completely relaxing the conscious mind is the trick. It is a bit like giving an instruction to your unconscious mind and thinking, "Oh well, it doesn't matter if it doesn't come up with the goods." This may feel a bit unsafe and a long way from how you would normally approach something, especially if you are an achiever. If you think back though, you will notice that whenever you have given up on something, it suddenly worked out. If that something was a person, they suddenly changed. You can also give your subconscious definite commands, especially if you are intent on achieving something of importance.

Visualisation

So many books tell you to visualise, but what does that mean? Does it mean that you sit in meditation and run a visual film? That is fine but I know very few people who have pulled that off. Most people start off okay, but they have not got the patience to keep going. Or they get mixed up with wondering what is required of them without being able to link it to everyday living. Visualisation is a bit like meditation. In my workbook I give you examples of what I have seen work, but it is a good idea to do it in your own way.

If visualising is difficult for you, you need to use your mind in the way you always do when you want something. This will work for you because it is familiar and because you are already doing it. This is also how your unconscious mind will work because it is used to receiving instructions from you this way. You could also tell others of your plans and make sure your unconscious is listening in and hears you talking about what you want. Always focus on what you do want. If what you do not want comes up, acknowledge the thoughts, let them through and breathe until you are calm. It is just your unconscious clearing out what it does not want, to make sure you get what you do want.

If you are auditory and your inner chatterbox keeps telling you that you will not succeed, let it talk until it gets bored and finally dries up. You could try changing its voice tone or pitch into a ridiculous voice and moving the voice right down into your big toe or around the back of your head. If it still does not dry up, get some psychic healing or ring a friend and keep on telling them why it will not work.

You will need your mind to remain calm when visualising. Visualising works well when you make the pictures bright and colourful and bring them nearer to you. If you do not want something or someone, make the pictures smaller, further away, colour them grey, then make them transparent and finally fade them away.

If you wish to become a more confident psychic think about other times when you felt confident. We all have these memories even if they consist of only a fleeting moment doing something really simple. Confidence is a must for anything in life, not just for developing as a psychic. Think about this for a moment. If you were as confident as you would like to be, how would you walk? How would you talk? In what tone of voice would you talk? What would your posture look like? Would you be slimmer? What kind of foods would you eat? What kind of people would you mix with? How would you look? What kind of clothes would you wear?

Practice walking with an air of confidence and notice how you would enter a room, perhaps with your head held high. Try smiling. When we look up and smile, our body reacts positively and coaxes our mind into thinking it is happy and confident. Never mind if it is not there yet, just pretend until it is. Pretend you have something of worth to offer people. Pretend you are liked. Imagine what your life would be like if absolutely *everyone* you know liked you? Keep thinking about this and as you do, tell and show your subconscious that this is what you want. If you add a feeling it will become doubly effective.

Analysing Every Detail

Your subconscious operates through dreams and symbols so it helps to be able to accept symbolic forms when they appear, even if they do not make sense. I clearly remember being able to accept whatever my mind brought to me much more so than other trainee psychics who felt the need to continue asking questions. I have often thought that most humans are far too complicated. I also believe that it is the state of "acceptance" that will prove immeasurably helpful for you to develop psychically. If you analyse every step of the way, you will tangle yourself up in the four per cent of your conscious mind, overlook the 96 per cent of your subconscious mind and slow yourself down. We want your conscious mind clear and in a good mental state to be able to give clear instructions to your subconscious.

If you know you are analytical by nature, satisfy your logical mind as soon as you can with answers to its questions. Give it proof of past experiences if it doubts and reassurance it if it is confused. Then allow it to rest. Train it to think clearly by giving it clear instructions. The mind is like a child. It needs coaxing and it needs to be given a direction. Too much discipline will cause it to rebel so constantly lead it in the direction you want it to go but in a gentle way. Continually show it what you do want, rather than what you do not want. If what you do not want keeps coming up, write it all down on a piece of paper and burn it. That way your mind will gradually become more positive and feel safe. It will then become your faithful servant quite able to do its job of instructing the subconscious.

Eccentricity

Being a bit eccentric has helped me enormously to channel, as so many messages can come through in symbolic form or dreams. When psychic messages come through, you will need to be very open-minded as Spirit can convey messages in unusual ways. They often use methods of communication way outside of my conscious awareness. I have even known people's lives to change merely because they phoned me and left a message. Even without hearing the message they experienced a sudden healing or their lives changed for the better. On occasion these events could be described as small miracles. By making the call, does the person's soul put a command out to the universe? Perhaps Spirit connects energies in the higher realms to invoke a healing. Who knows?

I do not really know how it works a lot of the time, but what I do know is that "acceptance" is the key to allowing these wonderful higher beings to work in a way that suits them. I also know that they will use you more if you allow them freedom of movement.

Lastly, in your vast unconscious memory banks, you may have been a psychic or a medium before. You may sense this and you may have all the knowledge necessary to start again locked deeply within. If this resonates with you, put a command out to your unconscious to access that past knowledge and hey presto, you will be a remarkably accurate psychic again. All that knowledge will come pouring back in. If you have been a medium in a former time, the same thing will happen providing there are no psychic blockages to overcome. This is what happened to Marjorie and Sarah. Marjorie realised, but Sarah did not and she was not even looking to become psychic.

Psychic Preparation

If you are a naturally organised person, you will have a head start here. If you are consistently searching for keys, taking too long thinking about what to wear, looking for your shoes, etc, you will come to realise that although there is nothing wrong with this, disorganisation takes up valuable time. The biggest block to developing psychically is a disorganised mind and a disorganised life. If you live in a constant state of mess or unfinished business, you will not notice the subtle messages and directions coming from your Higher Self or Spirit. Psychic ability is the moment-to-moment relay between you, your intuition, your Higher Self and the angels or Spirit. For this to happen, you will need to be able to reflect before giving a message.

Organisation is the outcome of clear thinking. Psychic guidance is the by-product of organisation. Frantic people have a low sense of self-awareness because they do not have time to listen to their inner impressions. Their chaos shuts down their intuition.

If you unclog any disorganisation, you will prepare yourself for the new to come in. When Lucy cleared her house out after many years of accumulation of old furniture, old clothes, unread newspapers and magazines and over a year's work of outstanding paperwork, she found the time to look at her astrology books. Within weeks she was being asked to lecture at the local school. You could call this a coincidence, but Dr Carl Jung describes it as synchronicity. Either way it is energy moving in a particular direction. Lucy's clearing out created space for more to come in. She uncovered her astrology books and reacquainted herself with that knowledge.

When you are asked to do something urgent how many times have you found yourself going off in another direction and clearing out the paperwork, the house or the spare drawer? In fact it seems that you will do anything to put it off rather than get on with the task at hand. On these days you may surprisingly get a lot of "other" outstanding jobs done and marvel at your output. You may wonder why this happens and believe that you are not motivated or it is an effort to get on with the original idea. This is not so. This is no coincidence; it is synchronisation or a psychic preparation. Often a de-cluttering is necessary before you can fulfil what you set out to do.

Please bear this in mind the next time you beat yourself up over this and realise that it is an important part of the preparation. On occasion I have thought I was lazy or not understood why I had so much energy for one thing and not another, even though I wanted to do the very thing I seemed to be putting off. Once you have cleared the other things, it often opens up the space for everything to flow naturally.

Psychic Diary

A psychic diary will work wonders for you if you are a methodical, organised individual. If this does not appeal to you, do not bother, for you will come to see it as yet another task. It is important that you enjoy your psychic development. If keeping a diary becomes a chore, you will not keep it up. Instead, try to make mental notes of improvements, subtle signs and any messages you receive. If you like the idea of keeping a diary, record everything psychic that happens to you or those around you. All psychic impressions, impulses and coincidences are a useful source of knowledge upon which you can build.

Every small impression is important because some of them are so subtle that they can get overlooked. If you keep a regular record you will soon begin to realise just how many times the impressions are coming. This will help to build your confidence. Remember to keep an open mind for the messages and the methods of communication may be entirely different each time.

Psychic Observation

If you cannot remember any psychic impulses or think you would not recognise one if you had one, open up your consciousness and start to notice more. Notice the colour of the man's socks on the underground. The amount of baldness another man has. Notice the tone of a girl's speech, an accent of another. Listen to people's words. Watch how they move their bodies. After teaching yoga I knew a great deal about people's bodies by just watching them walk. I do not remember when I realised I could do this. It helped me enormously later when I began psychically healing and seeing auras and the information they contain.

I thought there was something wrong with me when, after one evening at a dance, I discovered that I could remember where most of the people in the room had been standing and what they were wearing. There were over four hundred people there and I remembered the tone of their voices, their skin, their energy and how they interacted and danced with each other. Later, when driving home, I mentioned some of these details to the people travelling in the car with me and I was surprised to learn that they had only noticed about one-tenth of what I had seen. My ability to observe and retain information has crept up over the years without my conscious knowledge. My memory has improved enormously. This just goes to show that it has nothing to do with age.

As you people-watch, imagine what their personality is like. Try to get an idea of what they do for a living. Look at their aura. What state is it in? Is it clean and crisp or murky and dull? What kind of attractor fields are dominating them? Are they angry attractor fields? Are they low self-esteem attractor fields? Are they healthy or not? Do they have a lot of vitality? You could check out your accuracy by asking people you have never met if you can do a guessing game. Creative arty people love this sort of thing so they will not mind.

You could also watch comedy, for comedians have subtle timing and work with energy, especially those in partnerships who have worked together for years. Watch television programmes with funerals and see if you can pick up spirit around them. A visit to a graveyard is also a good experience if you wish to work as a medium. Sit quietly and ask Spirit to come forward. Souls do gather in these places and the angel of death and his host of mighty angels is always guarding them. If you feel unsafe about this, then you will be carrying fear of Spirit or the dead which needs to be cleared. Take a good look at the chapters on psychic attack and psychic protection. It is your own fear that attracts the wrong kind of Spirit, nothing else.

Notice anything and everything. Every experience, no matter how small, counts. Make sure you also notice where your psychic impulses come from. Are the impulses coming from your subconscious and just floating into your mind? Are they telepathically coming from someone else because you are thinking about them, or from the higher realms, the angelic kingdoms, or spirit guides? If they are coming from spirit guides, are they your own personal guides or are they floating guides from the higher realms with special messages? Get a real sense of what is taking place.

It could be that human spirits which have passed over are giving you impressions. If that is the case can you see anyone or hear what they are saying to you? Can you feel them? Do you know who they are and for whom the message is being conveyed? Is it their voice you are hearing or are the messages coming through in your own voice?

Do the impressions come from outside you, within your head or are they "gut feelings" or "knowings"? Mostly I receive information through the left hand side of my head about two to three feet away. Sometimes it is a lot further. Occasionally it comes from that place of super consciousness and I am aware it is a very beautiful place. I wait, sometimes there is a pause and then I receive another wave of information with pauses in between. The pauses are important so it is vital that you are able to wait patiently. You may have to explain this to your enquirer and ask them to stay quiet whilst you read for them. Remember you are a receptor – this is the one profession in which you cannot "go out there" and "make it happen" at your speed. Well actually you can, but only if you incorporate the help of your Higher Self with a strong respectful command and so long as it is absolutely necessary to heal and free another.

Unless you have a drawn a very robust spirit to you with an urgent message to convey, the energy will gather pace and will come in gradually, sometimes in fits and starts. It settles when you are properly connected to the source of the psychic information. A word of caution: some spirit can be very impatient to come through and can overwhelm you energetically if you are not careful. This is especially more prominent in clairsentients. If that happens, to avoid the impact, just let it pass through you. It may stun you for a few seconds but you will be fine after. They can be very emotional or you could be dealing with the distress of a newly-departed spirit and the emotions of your client. Just because Spirit have passed over does not mean they are peaceful. They will still be carrying the energy vibrations from their lifetimes on Earth. If this happens, ask your hHgher Self and their Higher Self to tone it all down to a level you can handle.

If a number of spirits want to come through all at once, you will need to control the situation by asking them to come through one at a time. It can be like being in a busy market with lots of people trying to talk to you all at once from different families. This only ever occurs with souls that have passed over and to newly-developing mediums. Guides and angels are much more subtle in their approach especially those on the higher echelons.

You may find it easier to work with people who are not in the room with you, especially if you are doing psychic healing. This way you will not be distracted by their presence, their observation of you, or their energetic imbalances. You will find you will be able to read more accurately without these distractions. For some psychics, this simply does not work and they need the person in front of them to be able to read properly.

40

How to Choose a Good Psychic

When you visit or phone a psychic, what do you want to happen? Try to be clear about where you want the reading to go. When choosing a psychic you will need to feel relaxed and that it is "right." A good psychic will make you feel comfortable and will usually get straight to the point. If there is a muddle or confusion during the first few minutes, stop the reading – this can easily be done if you are on a psychic phone line. If not, say something to the psychic. It is important that you tell the truth. A good psychic will want feedback and if you are not happy, they need to know. It is truly remarkable how many people end up on my doorstep unhappy with readings they have previously received. I do not think it is the fault of the psychic reader, more a lack of proper communication or courage on the part of the enquirer to speak up. You need to make sure that you know and ask for what you want to avoid ambiguity.

Readings Are Open to Interpretation

A good psychic will not expect you to accept every word they say, as they realise that their readings are open to personal interpretation and that you have free will. What is more, some of what they say may have already happened. If they labour in the past too much, stop them and tell them you want to know about the future. Some of them get stuck in a rut of repeating themselves. I have known many people who end difficult relationships directly after a psychic reading because they were at last able to understand the dire consequences of what would happen if they stayed. A reading does not mean that you absolutely must live by what is said. It is merely an indication of what is in store for you. In other words, the outcome if you continue down the road you are going.

A good psychic will be diplomatic about how any uncomfortable information is passed on to you. If you are sensitive or highly-strung, an experienced psychic will adopt an approach that will work for you. He or she will know you are sensitive as this is part of their job. Sometimes, news of a death will emerge and, as we are all different, each psychic will approach this differently. Any news can be conveyed if it is done kindly and warmly.

Poorly-developed psychics can be brutal in their renditions and this may cause someone to panic and mistake the nature of the information coming through. Such a psychic might also confuse his or her own issues with yours, project their problems onto you and misguide you. They can be forthright and judgmental. If you have attracted this, look at why and where you have problems with authority figures. If what they are saying does not feel right, stop them to get clarification and a sense of their personality. Are they bossy? Do they read in a way that leaves no room for you to manoeuvre?

Some psychics do not like general readings while others thrive on them. We all fall into different categories. There are times in your life when you will need the "bigger picture" and a greater long-term vision, and other times when you will need to hear about the specific details. Psychics fall into different categories. Some can seem very "out there" and channel the high spiritual vision and long-term soul outcomes. Other, more down-to-Earth types, will tell you about the gossip down the road and what someone had for dinner last night at 8.15pm. I always begin my readings wanting to know exactly what my enquirer wants to hear and what they wish to achieve. I suppose that makes me pretty specific. Often he or she wants healing for a family member or the unraveling of a concern that they have not been able to resolve. They are often disinterested in clairvoyance for the future.

Making Assumptions

I recently misjudged an elderly lady at an exhibition. She was going towards an older generation medium, but she then did a complete "U-turn" and suddenly turned up at my stand. I wondered why. I had thought the other medium was perfect for her. When I asked her what she needed she said she wanted a deep healing for her daughter and her son, which would involve in-depth past life knowledge, an area the other medium was not qualified in. She told me that she absolutely "knew" she had to speak to me. Do you see now how we can make mistakes? My own conditioning had her "boxed" into a specific set up. I was labeling her.

A good psychic will not clock-watch and usher you out on the dot. This way you will be free to ask questions and get clarification of what is taking place. A good psychic will be clear with her or his statements and you will feel a sense of well-being at the end of your reading. If you leave in a state of doubt or concern, ask the psychic or medium for more clarity. Some psychics give recordings of their readings and others do not. Having your reading recorded is entirely up to you. I have not found it to prove very useful when doing a reading and a healing, but a very good idea when giving past life readings or clairvoyance. Try not to talk too much to the psychic or medium or else you will distract them.

Word of mouth is probably the best way of finding the right psychic for you. Remember though that the psychic who was perfect for your best friend may not be as accurate for you. People turn up at my door because they tell me they "know" they must come to see me. I have been told that they see something in my photograph. To sum up, you are looking for a warm, generous, compassionate, accurate, highly-skilled psychic. I have met quite a number of excellent psychics and mediums who certainly fit these criteria.

41

Become a True Professional

As you progress your psychic training, you may find you need to widen your knowledge. Some readings can be complex and you will be able to draw upon knowledge more readily if you already have it stored within you. Spirit and your Higher Self will find it easier to work through you if you have considerable reserves to draw upon. When I began writing, I did a great deal of research. This encouraged me to read a lot of different books on metaphysics and spirituality. I noticed that the quality of my readings was greatly enhanced because of my new-found knowledge. I would receive impressions from the Angelic Spirit Kingdom and the Elementals simply because I knew more about their existence. I was able to give more information about past lives when I had watched a very interesting historical series of television programmes about the past.

On a number of occasions I have heard people complain about psychics who seem to give the same reading to everyone they meet. I hope this will not apply to you. If it does and you find you repeat yourself, it needs to be psychically cleared and healed. That way you will expand your consciousness and the horizons of those who come to you for guidance.

Psychic Junkies

Some people who are depressed or lacking in inner strength flit from psychic to psychic hoping these people can tell them something exciting to lift their dreary lives. They hand over the responsibility of sorting out their entire life to another person. If they receive a good message they are temporarily uplifted and then, when nothing of any significance happens, they slump back down even lower than before. They then seek another medium or psychic and repeat the same pattern. Be careful if you come up against one of these individuals, for they are unrealistic and you can easily be made into a part of their fantasy. Beware also of anyone who tries to put you on a pedestal. If you see this happening then it is time for a psychic healing to disperse this type of energy and find out why you attracted this. People who do this tend to have an overzealous "need" to connect with you. Whenever someone puts you on a pedestal, the chances are that the same person is going to knock you off the golden throne the instant that reality kicks in, for instance, when they realise that you are not perfect and you will fall with a nasty bump. I know because this has happened to me. It is essential that you stay free of all of these energy projections.

Getting it Right

Many people assume that you are going to "hit the spot" when they come for a reading – their specific "spot" that is. You might not have a clue that this "specific spot" exists until they land you with it at the end, inferring that you have not done a good job. This does not mean that you are inadequate or a terrible psychic, but that they have a very "fixed" idea of exactly what is going to take place. They might assume that you will definitely bring their long lost great grandmother through, who went gold mining in the outback of Australia, or their potential lover over thirty years ago whom they are still yearning for. Failing that, it will be the exact member of family they wish to speak with in Spirit, or that they are finally going to meet their soul mate, or win a large sum of money from the lottery.

However, spiritual readings do not work that way. Spirit often does not adhere to our wishes as we would like. A completely different member of the family may be brought forward instead of the one they had hoped for. This can upset some people, but you now know what you need to do. Stick to your guns, stay neutral and keep going. The family member who has been brought through will be there for a very definite reason and your client needs to understand and listen or they could lose valuable insight.

Take Control

You could also waste a lot of your valuable time and energy by giving your client excellent information, thinking you are helping them in this way. However, I can assure you that if the information is not the "exact" information they were seeking or the "exact" idea they had conjured up, they will discard it and you will have wasted your time. If this happens your client will not thank you, but rather they will complain. Another irritation for a medium is that many people drop in the "all important question" right at the end of their reading, leading you to continue way past your time limit. This is fine now and again, but if you consistently do this you will grow tired and you could end up feeling resentful, working two or three times as hard as you should be. This is devastating for your vitality.

Be strong at the beginning and insist that they give you several major starting points. If there are too many, make it clear that you will not have time to cover all of those points and ask them to reduce the list to the important points only. I once had a friend who worked as an animal healer and her enquirer presented her with twenty-seven questions about her cat. If your client is a chatterbox, create the quiet space at the beginning of your reading. You can either pause periodically and ask if there is anything they want to ask, or you can give them the option of asking perhaps three questions at the end. Either way you will need to keep them quiet. If they keep talking, make it clear that they are paying for your time and wasting theirs.

Hold Your Own

I have not told you that the psychic pathway is easy, because it is not. Most good psychics and mediums will tell you that they are constantly learning. When people hear that you are psychic, you will get very different reactions. One person may instantly request that you tell them their life story, while another might tell you that it is all mumbo-jumbo. Someone else may begin to treat you with suspicion.

I remember a colleague of mine at the gym feeling sorry for me because she felt I was "so not mainstream." Again, if this occurs, that all important place of neutrality needs to emerge from within you. You must be completely untouched by their views. I used to grow irritated by cynics and skeptics and as a result I always tried to prove myself. I now know how to remain diplomatic and simply move on. People are entitled to their point of view and I don't "throw pearls amongst swine."

Do Not Waste Your Time

If people instantly want your attention, slow them down and ask them to book an appointment with you; otherwise you may squander your energies. Be careful, as sooner or later you will scatter yourself too thinly and wear yourself out. You also will not be taken seriously and people will expect freebies whenever they see you. What is more they will tell their friends and keep ringing and asking you for even more free readings. If they have to make an appointment, journey to see you, or pay the telephone bill to listen to what you have to say, they will value you. You will also be working in your own space with a clean bright aura ready to bring messages through inside a firm structure.

Stay on time, as if you keep running over it could indicate a need to please. Being late is unprofessional and generally people don't like it. Remember too that you will accomplish a better reading if you stick to the point at the beginning of the reading.

Asking someone one or two questions at the beginning doesn't mean that you "can't do it." It just means you are making sure that you go in the right direction.

All the psychics I know are good at being curious. Many of them have Scorpio rising in their astrological charts, which means they have detective-like minds that thrive on investigation. They usually have a laser ability to delve in and root out the cause of the issues. You often hear them say, "I need to get to the bottom of this." This is the type of curiosity that will stand you in good stead. On the other hand you may be quite the opposite; passive and very accepting. This will also work well as you will allow your spiritual brothers and sisters in the invisible world to do their job properly through you.

Either way it will work. The most important thing is to be yourself and work with the method that is right for you. This is very individual stuff. If you yearn for the gifts and skills of another medium or psychic, another psychic block clearance is on the cards so you can stop comparing yourself, clear your inadequacy and allow your own way of working to emerge.

Having a healthy interest in what makes another person "tick" is also essential to becoming a good psychic, backed up by a strong empathy and caring for their welfare. On a number of occasions I have been to talks by eminent people who appear to have "worn themselves out." They do not want to work anymore and it shows. Steer clear of this type of thing if you come across it. Some of them are still treading the boards because they do not have enough money to sustain them. Instead of retiring, they have to keep on long past their energetic and enthusiastic sell-by date. Elvis Presley fell into this category because of his constant need for acclaim. He literally worked himself to death.

42

The End of Your Journey

Some time has passed since you arrived at my house for your reading. I hope that many of your questions about becoming psychic have now been answered. I sincerely hope that you are now feeling more confident about progressing psychically and growing spiritually. Remember to tune into yourself and discover how far you want to take your psychic development studies. Listen to your heart, as that way you will link directly into your soul and get the answers to most of your questions. You can also use my Home Study Course to help you further, in which I will train you personally. Psychic Development Workshops are also available together with a selection of MP3s to heal you.

About the Author

Molly Ann Fairley is a psychic, medium, teacher and healer. She travels the UK, Ireland and Europe teaching psychic awareness, psychic healing and psychic self-clearing.

Numerous articles have been written about her work, which include psychic healing for slimming. She has produced The Slimming Journey on CD and her unique self-help Psychic Slimming cards for those wishing to take a holistic approach to weight loss.

She is currently writing a psychic development home study course and psychic healing cards. She is also one of the contributors of the self-empowerment book, *The Light*, to help people reawaken their inner Light.

227

Products

These products are available to enhance your spiritual journey, whether that journey be to develop psychically, or to lose excess weight.

'Karmic Angel' CDs
You can approach The Lords of Karma and ask to have your karma cancelled. This CD will show you how.

Books
The Light
22 authors have come together from across the globe to empower people and transform their lives. The goal is to raise $1 million for 7 different charities. I am one of the contributing authors.

Psychic Slimming Booklet
The booklet will call upon Spirit to answer questions about your weight issue and so help to put your mind at rest.

Psychic Essences
Made from a natural combination of oils, these essences will protect, heal and aid your psychic development.

Psychic Slimming Essences
All made with natural oil combinations these essences act as powerful slimming aids.

Psychic Slimming Cards
Embedded in these powerful Psychic Healing Cards are Divine messages to enable you to slim.

The cards expose your issue and give you practical help on how to heal it.

Spiritual Weight Loss CDs
'A Slimming Journey' has been recorded to guide you every step of the way on your weight loss plan. Individual CDs are also available for comfort eating, binging and sugar addictions.

For information on Psychic Development Courses, Psychic Healing Courses and Training, Personal Readings and the Healing Circle please contact Molly Ann on 0044 208 541 3084 or www.theschoolofpsychicstudies.co.uk

Lightning Source UK Ltd.
Milton Keynes UK
UKOW04f1221190615

253788UK00002B/18/P